Entrepreneurship

The entrepreneur has been neglected over the years in formal economic theorizing. Previously there has been only eclectic theories, such as human capital theory and network dynamics which discuss certain aspects of entrepreneurial behaviour. This book closes a gap in the entrepreneurship literature.

Inspired by modern physics, the author brings together an evolutionary methodology, along the way implicating quantum, graph and percolation theory. This book provides an interdisciplinary approach to entrepreneurship, opening up new ideas in modelling:

- how to structure economic thinking in an easy way
- how to implement new ideas into a simulation study
- how to balance line modelling procedures with stylised facts.

Thomas Grebel has provided a synthesis of all the main theories of entrepreneurship and the original thinking within this book should be of interest to all those working in the area of business and management as well as economics.

Thomas Grebel is lecturer in Economics at the University of Augsburg, Germany.

Studies in Global Competition

A series of books edited by John Cantwell, The University of Reading, UK and David Mowery, University of California, Berkeley, USA

Entrepreneurship

A New Perspective

Thomas Grebel

London and New York

First published 2004 by Routledge
11 New Fetter Lane, London EC4P 4EE

Simultaneously published in the USA and Canada
by Routledge
29 West 35th Street, New York, NY 10001

Routledge is an imprint of the Taylor & Francis Group

© 2004 Thomas Grebel

Printed and bound in Great Britain by MPG Books Ltd, Bodmin

British Library Cataloguing in Publication Data
A catalogue record for this book is available from the British Library

Library of Congress Cataloging in Publication Data
A catalog record of this book has been requested

ISBN 0-415-34118-3

Contents

Figures

Plan of Book

The entrepreneur has always been a pivotal point in economic history. His importance has never been in doubt – neither in politics nor in economics. Indeed, there is evidence that a high level of entrepreneurship creates jobs, economic growth and, hence, welfare. It is the entrepreneur, a man of action, a heroic person, who is the key element of economic prosperity. Turning to economic theory, however, specifically to orthodox economic theory, the entrepreneur has gradually been deprived from that central position in the economy. Due to the need for a consistent, normative theory in economics, in order to explain the optimal allocation of scarce resources rather than to consider the specificities of human behavior that may prevent (support) them from (in) doing so, the entrepreneur was eventually knocked off his pedestal and made way for a methodologically robust figure: the Homo economicus, a dispassionate seeker of efficiency, a playmate of the methodological treatment.

In this work, the story of the entrepreneur in economic theory is briefly retraced. Furthermore, a methodological discussion will provide a sound underpinning for a model of entrepreneurial behavior. Thereby, it also tries to bridge the missing link in economics and bring psychological and sociological aspects into economic theorizing. Therefore, this book is divided into three major parts. Part I delivers an overview of the literature on entrepreneurship. Part II takes up the methodological discussion about a basic evolutionary setting. Part III rounds off the work with an evolutionary model on entrepreneurship.

The historical sketch (part I) starts with eclectic ideas and the basic intuition on the role of the entrepreneur. A collection of possible functions and qualities of the entrepreneur is given at the beginning. Very early, the French School delivers lots of insights into entrepreneurial functions. The Classical School rather puts its focus on capital than on the entrepreneur. With the neoclassical era entrepreneurs have become gradually eradicated, when the Newtonian mechanics were introduced in economic theorizing;

methodology smothered the tiniest contingencies of entrepreneurial actions in theory. Due to the Austrian School, the entrepreneur was revived
to stress his important position within the economic process. Despite the
contributions it made to neoclassical methodology, the Austrian tradition
initiated also a critical discussion of such methodology. Schumpeter criticized the incapability of equilibrium analysis to substantiate the innovation
process as a fundamental element of economic change. The endogenous
element, Schumpeter put forth, is the entrepreneur, who pushes through
new combinations, i.e. innovations, and destructs any kind of presumed
state of optimality, which, quite contrarily, might never come into existence. Kirzner sought the entrepreneur in disequilibrium but in contrast to
Schumpeter, he did not refrain from a final state of equilibrium. Knight
discussed the idea of a parameterizable uncertainty, and came to the conclusion that there is the differentiation of true uncertainty which does not
allow for any prediction, a state of economic ignorance which only an
entrepreneur dares to cope with. But none of those economists build a
framework to suitably incorporate the entrepreneur as a coherent feature
into economic analysis. There was just the notion of an alternative approach. It was the term evolutionary, which was meant to summarize all
heterodoxy in economic analysis contrasting some neoclassical shortcomings. Not surprisingly, evolutionary economics rather became the allegory
of economists' yearning for a standardizing body to tackle economic phenomena which had been reduced to negligible side effects in the neoclassical economic process.

Consequently, the history of evolutionary economics is outlined in the
second part leading into a discussion about the philosophy of science. The
parallels between natural sciences, philosophy and social sciences point
out the thread of rationality through all sciences suggesting a deterministic view of the world. Taking into account the facts of observable data,
empiricism likewise followed determinism. Even the reconciliation between both, rationalism and empiricism, did not give up a deterministic
world view. In the 20th century, the findings in physics, such as in thermodynamics and especially in quantum physics, suggested accepting some
indeterminism in nature; an idea that puts into perspective normative theories as well as predictability; an unpleasant constraint for scientific research in general and a fundamental critique on neoclassical economics
in particular. Hitherto, however, indeterminism also turned out to puzzle
evolutionary economists. The discussion in part II ends with a systematic
methodological framework adapting Heisenberg's uncertainty principle to
economic behavior in general and entrepreneurial behavior specifically.

In part III, the core element of this book, the model of entrepreneurial
behavior, is gradually introduced. The pivotal point is the bounded rationality of actors, whereby the bimodal ontology of the human mind, being

a part of reality as well as an actively creative element of reality, serves as a theoretical basis. Therefore, the psychology of actors is laid out. A static perspective of the human cognition process, with regard to human understanding and processing of new information and knowledge subject to limited absorptive capacities, is developed. New technological knowledge has to be absorbed by actors in the first place. Not before actors understand the principles of a new technology, such as the functioning of the internet, they become potential innovators in commercializing a new technology. Since the diffusion of knowledge is an indeterministic process, it cannot be modeled analytically. Therefore, percolation theory will serve as a metaphor and, apart from that, it will be used as a tool to implement this idea into the complete model at the end of this book. Furthermore, the sociological aspect of actors' psychology is introduced, since the mere understanding of a technology does not automatically make an entrepreneur out of actors. Decisions are made within a certain context. Individuals might hesitate to run a business all by themselves, but might do so when being supported by friends. In contrast to the behavior of the Homo economicus there is symmetry-breaking in human behavior. This is one of the outcomes of part II which is taken up on. Apart from what an actor's friends believe, the overall evaluation of a new technology by actors in general is crucial for entrepreneurial behavior. If the economic potential of a technology is positively evaluated by actors, some are likely to engage in entrepreneurial actions anticipating future economic developments. It is the shared mental model of actors, influenced by socio-economic indicators on new technologies and their economic applications that make actors confident of future prosperity. Once actors are informed about a new technology and form a positive attitude towards its economic applicability, they are activated in terms of entrepreneurial actions. If the general attitude of actors is in favor of a new technology, actors who understand a new technology and therefore are able to innovate on that technology (such as opening up a bookstore on the internet), they start to engage in a networking process (chapter 8). In case all contingencies coincide, some actors happen to come together at a certain point in time and decide to found a firm. Conclusively, the basic findings in the entrepreneurship literature (part I) and the meta-theoretical reflections delivering a methodological foundation (part II), are brought together in part III. Thus, the characteristics of bounded rational actors with an economic behavior subject to individual, sociological and some indeterministic facts become the driving forces of entrepreneurial behavior. The results of the model meet stylized facts, so that eventually a consistent evolutionary model of entrepreneurial behavior based on a sound methodological framework is developed.

Acknowledgments

This book would have never been possible without the support of many people.

First of all, I want to thank my family: my parents and grandparents who raised me in free thinking and making autonomous decisions; my brothers with their wives, and my sister just for being there. Furthermore, I am very grateful to my friends who managed to boost my motivation at harder times: Gerhard Ilg who discussed many drafts with me, Karoline Strobl who never shied away from discussing details important to me, Rüdiger Przybilla, my companion in writing his thesis, too. Hansjörg and Alexander Durz all along with Lukas S. Schimpfle who spurred my entrepreneurial spirit from a practical point of view. Thomas Konopka, Bastian Walcher and many more wonderful musicians I share the passion for music in my spare time.

Many thanks also to my colleagues who have always been helpful and understanding: Markus Balzat, who spent a lot of time discussing improvements of my work and Andreas Pyka who got me started in simulation studies. Thanks to Monika Bredow, our secretary, and to many other colleagues from our economics department. In particular, I am very much indebted to Professor Dr. Horst Hanusch who gave me plenty of scope to do research and thus made this book possible in the first place. Arnold Wentzel from the Rand Afrikaans University in South Africa I thank for his proof-reading and his valuable comments.

Last but not least, I want to thank Uwe Cantner. He has been giving me a lot of guidance ever since we met. He always knew how to open up my mind and provoke a creative way of thinking. Uwe and Fabienne, his daughter, have become close friends to me.

List of Symbols

δ delimiter of a firm's burning rate

ε degree of agents' bounded rationality

η price elasticity of demand

$\frac{W}{P}$ real wage rate

Γ lag operator

κ_i absorptive capacity of agent i

ϕ minimal fraction of an agent's direct network members with a common specificity

π_{jt} profit of firm j at time t

Ψ founding threshold

ρ persistence of a shock on output

$\sharp$ number

τ transferrable (non-tacit) knowledge

$\varphi(t)$ sustainable growth rate

$\vec{a}$ vector

a_i agent i

AD_t aggregate demand at time t

AS_t aggregate supply at time t

b	rate of knowledge diffusion
c_{j0}	numeraire of unit variable costs
ce_{qt}	comprehensive endowments of group q at time t
D_e	diffusivity
E	set of edges (connections)
e_{ij}	edge between vertex i and j
es_i	entrepreneurial spirit of agent i
ex_t	number of exits at time t
F_t^{new}	set of new firms at time t
f_{jt}	actual firm
G	effective elastic moduli
g	time parameter
g_e	effective electrical conductivity
$H(x)$	heavyside function
h_{jt}	oligopolistic interdependence of firm j at time t
hc_i	human capital of agent i
inc_t	number of incumbent firms at time t
K	production factor capital
k	number of connections (ties between agents)
K_j^t	firm's total cost curve at time t
K_{jt}^{fix}	fixed costs
k_{jt}^{var}	variable unit costs
L	production factor labor
l_t	units of production factor labor employed in equilibrium at time t
LD_t	labor demand at time t
lr	learning rate

LS_t	labor supply at time t
M	size of s system
m	number of temporarily potential firms
N	agents in the neighborhood
n	number of elements
N_i	neighborhood of agent i
n_t	number of firms at time t
P	nominal price
p	probability of a site being occupied
$P(p)$	percolation probability
p_{cb}	percolation threshold in the case of bond percolation
p_{cs}	percolation threshold in the case of site percolation
p_{jt}	product price of firm j at time t
$p_{jt}^{planned}$	planned priced of firm j at time t
PF_t	production function at time t
PF_t	set of potential firms at time $t=0$
pf_{qt}	potential firm at time $t=0$
pf_{qt}	potential firm's evaluated comprehensive endowment
q	agents of a k-group that constitute a potential firm
ru_t	positive return on sales
S	a system
s	number of distinct n-systems
$S(A)$	adjacency matrix of a system
$S_p(p)$	average number of clusters of size s
t	time index
u_t	growth rate of sector sales at time t

V	set of vertices (agents)
vc_i	venture capital of agent i
W	nominal wages
w_i	angent i's stock of novel knowledge
$X^A(p)$	accessible fraction
X^B	backbone fraction
$x_{exit,t}$	total turnover of exiting firms at time t
x_{jt}	output of firm j at time t
x_{jt}^{cum}	accumulated output of firm j at time t
$x_{jt}^{planned}$	planned output of firm j at time t
$x_{surv,t}$	total turnover of surviving firms at time t
$xi_p(p)$	correlation length
Y	total output
y_{jt}	price limit of firm j at time t
GPT	general purpose technology

Part I

The Critical Path of the Entrepreneur in Economic Theory

1 A Historical Sketch of the Research on Entrepreneurship

The analysis of entrepreneurship has been one of the most challenging subjects in the history of economic analysis. Research on entrepreneurship is as old as economic analysis itself. The importance of entrepreneurs in economy has always been emphasized but it has never come as far as to be develop into a consistent and comprehensive theory on entrepreneurship. Why is that? When doing research on entrepreneurship, almost every economist comes to a point where he wonders whether the entrepreneur does not fit into orthodox economic analysis or, vice versa, orthodox economic analysis is not able to explain the phenomenon of the entrepreneur. The literature on economic behavior seems to comprise of a nearly holistic approach to the understanding of humankind's way of dealing with scarce resources. The literature on entrepreneurship, however, is eclectic and almost fails to track the quintessence of entrepreneurial behavior.

When we talk about entrepreneurship, we talk about assumptional frameworks, how to treat uncertainty, knowledge, rationality, etc.; and on top of it, we talk about methodology. This is what makes it very difficult to tell a distinct story about the entrepreneur leaving aside such kind of seemingly secondary aspects.

This part gives an overview on the work that has already been done on the topic of entrepreneurship in the economic literature and, furthermore, the attempt is made to categorize literature in order to track the development of the different strands of thought leading to different paradigms in economic analysis and thus determine the apparently symptomatic treatment of the entrepreneur.

1.1 The Pre-Neoclassics

It is not obvious at all where the actual starting point to analyze entrepreneurship is found. When we look at the literature there are various suggestions how to approach entrepreneurship.[1] Casson (1990) provides a fourfold division of entrepreneurship approaches: some focus on the factor distribution of income, some investigate the entrepreneur's role within the market process, others focus on a *heroic* Schumpeter vision and the fourth group analyzes the entrepreneur in the context of a firm. Nevertheless, the entrepreneur's origin, his economic identity and his distinct economic role is still puzzling. Hébert and Link (1982) assorted various "themes" which differentiations, concerning the entrepreneur's role, have been put forward in economic literature:

1. *The entrepreneur is the person who assumes the risk associated with uncertainty (e.g., Cantillon, Thünen, Mangoldt, Mill, Hawley, Knight, Mises, Cole, Shackle).*

2. *The entrepreneur is the person who supplies financial capital (e.g., Smith, Turgot, Böhm-Bawerk, Edgeworth, Pigou, Mises).*

3. *The entrepreneur is an innovator (e.g., Baudeau, Bentham, Thünen, Schmoller, Sombart, Weber, Schumpeter).*

4. *The entrepreneur is a decision maker (e.g., Cantillon, Menger, Marshall, Wieser, Amasa Walker, Francis Walker, Keynes, Mises, Shackle, Cole, Schultz).*

5. *The entrepreneur is an industrial leader (e.g., Say, Saint-Simon, Amasa Walker, Francis Walker, Marshall, Wieser, Sombart, Weber, Schumpeter).*

6. *The entrepreneur is a manager or superintendent (e.g., Say, Mill, Marshall, Menger).*

7. *The entrepreneur is an organizer and coordinator of economic resources (e.g., Say, Walras, Wieser, Schmoller, Sombart, Weber, Clark, Davenport, Schumpeter, Coase).*

8. *The entrepreneur is the owner of an enterprise (e.g., Quesnay, Wieser, Pigou, Hawley).*

9. *The entrepreneur is an employer of factors of production (e.g., Amasa Walker, Francis Walker, Wieser, Keynes).*

10. *The entrepreneur is a contractor (e.g., Bentham).*

11. *The entrepreneur is an arbitrageur (e.g., Cantillon, Walras, Kirzner).*

12. *The entrepreneur is an allocator of resources among alternative uses (e.g., Cantillon, Kirzner, Schultz).*[2]

Besides the literature explicitly focusing on entrepreneurship, the related literature is so huge that almost every subject in economic analysis is touched. So the entrepreneurial element becomes a prevailing element within the economic realm. Nevertheless, it has to be stated that the discussion, as done in orthodox theory, can also be lead without referring to the entrepreneur at all; and paradoxically, the entrepreneurial element decreases to a minor economic phenomenon not considered necessary to be taken into account.

Owing to the elusiveness of the entrepreneur within orthodox economic theory, a brief historical sketch will help to trace back the origin and the paradigmatic development of the research on entrepreneurship in order to get into the discussion. Hébert and Link (1982), Casson (1982) and Barreto (1989) among others have already given a profound overview on the literature to be investigated.

Figure 1.1 depicts a possible categorization of economists that elaborated or touched on the entrepreneur in his work.

1.2 The French School

Richard Cantillon (1680s – 1734) Cantillon[3] has to be seen as the precursor of the research in entrepreneurship. Cantillon was renowned as a successful entrepreneur himself (to use this term in a colloquial sense). He described economic life at his time: *landowners* would lease their land to *farmers* and live on the rent they earn. A second group, the *hirelings*, are employees who earn a fixed amount of money. The third group of people Cantillon calls the *undertakers*; they take the entrepreneurial part in economic life. The specific feature Cantillon associated with the undertaker was the fact that they face a high degree of uncertainty. Consequently, all actors who produce or buy goods at a certain price and sell them for an uncertain price, thus earning an unfixed income, belong to the group of undertakers. Cantillon emphasized that the prominent quality of those undertakers is the willingness to deal with uncertainty.[4] They function as a medium to facilitate *exchange* and *circulation*. They coordinate, make decisions, engage in markets and connect producers with consumers.[5]

François Quesnay (1694 – 1774) Cantillon had a great influence on Quesnay's work. Quesnay was actually a physician employed by Louis XV. Inspired by Cantillon's idea of the *circular flow of income*, he used the analogy to the human blood circulation, which was also discovered in those days. This resulted in Quesnay's famous *Tableau Économique*, an analytical model which was the first mathematical model based on the general equilibrium concept. Quesnay has also become known as the leader of the so-called *Physiocrats*, a group of people whose ideas were based on the metaphor of nature.[6] Quesnay's as well as Cantillon's entrepreneurial vision was restricted to agriculture. Conclusively, Quesnay also divided eco-

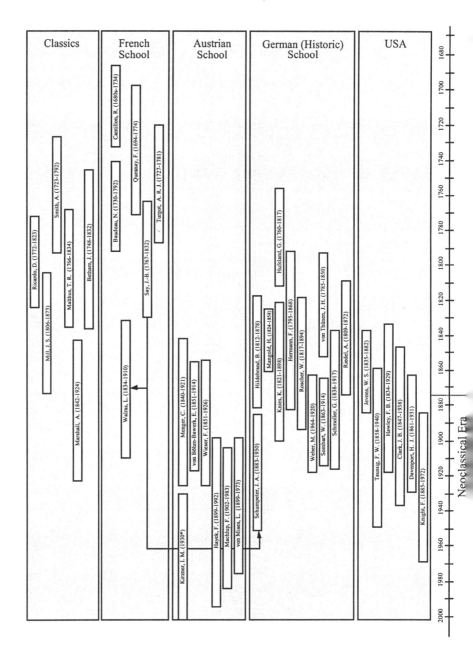

nomic actors into three groups adding some more specific qualities to these groups: the *landowners* he also called the *proprietary class* with property rights in land. The *farmers* he labeled the *productive class* capable to make profits and produce material for the third class, which is the *artisans* that manufacture goods. Quesnay was the first who brought the role of *capital* into the debate and pictured the entrepreneur as an *independent owner of a business.*[7] It is obvious that agriculture played a dominant role in economic analysis at that time so that the concept of the entrepreneur was not expanded beyond the agricultural sphere.

Nicolas Baudeau (1730 – 1792) Nicolas Baudeau was one of Quesnay's disciples. Furthermore, Cantillon's vision of the entrepreneur as a risk bearer also influenced Baudeau's ideas on entrepreneurship. Moreover, he contributed the idea of the entrepreneur as an innovator. He formulated the basic need of the entrepreneur to reduce his cost to increase his profits, an idea we nowadays call process innovation. Thus, he touched Schumpeter's theory on innovation and entrepreneurship. Besides, Baudeau stressed another important aspect that had already been put forward by Quesnay, that is, the importance of the individual's energy, knowledge and ability, which represent some of the determinants of economic success. These specific qualities provide the entrepreneur with the chance to control some aspects of the economic process whereas in terms of non-controllable aspects he puts himself at risk.[8]

Anne-Robert Jacques Turgot (1727 – 1781) Turgot's work delivered a footing for a large field in economics. He initiated preliminary thoughts to the theory of utility, anticipating the concept of diminishing marginal utility. He generated a theory on value and money and finally a theory on capital, savings and interest which had a striking impact on his concept of the entrepreneur.[9] Turgot was finance minister of Louis XVI and therefore familiar with the importance of capital in economy. According to Turgot, the accumulation of wealth goes along with the accumulation of money, which is achieved by saving. Once economic agents accumulate money they become capitalists who can make investment decisions. Then, they are in the position to decide whether to buy land, to invest in a business or simply lend the capital to others. Consequently, Turgot's entrepreneur in the first place is a capitalist and may opt to either become a landowner, simply stay a capitalist as a pure lender, or become an entrepreneur. In Turgot's concept of the entrepreneur, the significance of capital dominates the entrepreneurial role. The entrepreneur is a *capitalist–entrepreneur* who seeks to earn interest on the capital invested and to obtain remuneration for his manpower.[10]

Jean-Baptiste Say (1767 – 1832) Jean-Baptiste Say accomplished a big step forward in two fields: not only did he deliver he the building blocks for economic theorizing still to come at that time, he also managed to integrate the entrepreneur into a complete system.[11] Concerning entrepreneurship, he was the first to solidify the entrepreneur as an independent economic agent who combines and coordinates productive factors. Thus, Say emphasized the functional role of the entrepreneur as a coordinator, as the active role within the economic process, which makes the entrepreneur unequivocally distinguishable from the capitalist, the landowner and the workman.[12] At the same time, Say's economic concept constitutes a pivotal point in economic analysis and provides the foundation for various schools of thought. It bears the notion of general *equilibrium theory* and, in a larger sense, of the *Neoclassical School*. Apart from that, he puts the entrepreneur, as a coordinator, on top of the market process making it a story of the *Austrian School*. In addition, Say describes the entrepreneur's specific qualities foreshadowing the heroic Schumpeterian vision of the entrepreneur. Say marks the bifurcation point between orthodox and heterodox economics. To be more precise, it is necessary to set forth the basic ideas of Say's theory of production and distribution. Following Barreto (1989), figure 1.2 shows Say's production system. There are three fundamental production factors Say calls *capital, human industry* and *natural agents*. The underlying capital concept contains real capital as well as monetary capital. The natural agents enclose the entire nature with the resources it supplies and the laws it is guided by. These three factors are combined to produce *final goods*. However, Say decomposes the *human industry* into three subgroups: *philosophers, workmen* and *entrepreneurs*. Correspondingly, the production process is divided into the following steps: before a *final good* can be produced, one has to study *"(...) the laws and conduct of nature (...)"*.[13] In other words, a functional part of human industry is the task to generate the necessary technological knowledge to produce a tradable good. The next step is to launch and coordinate the production process which will be executed in the third step by a workman. The generation of knowledge is done by a *philosopher* that elaborates a *theory* which then finds its *application* through the entrepreneur who coordinates the whole production process, which eventually is *executed* by the workman. The entrepreneur commands, supervises and coordinates the whole system. If the entrepreneur is left out in Say's production system, the economic process will come to a halt. Barreto (1989)[14] calls him a *central processing unit*, Hébert and Link (1982)[15] call him a *catalyst* to underline the importance of Say's entrepreneur. When we look at Say's distribution process in figure 1.3, the significant role of the entrepreneur comes even more obvious. Not only coordinates the entrepreneur the production process, he also takes the key role in income distribution. He pays the capitalist interest on the financial capital he borrowed; if not the entrepreneur himself is a capitalist. He pays rent for the *natural agents* and he recompenses the workman (philosopher) for the labor (knowledge) provided.

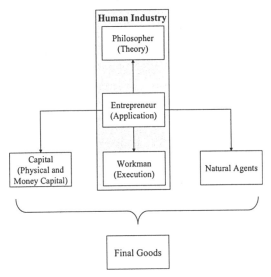

Figure 1.2: The production system of Jean-Baptiste Say.

The residual amount of the revenues gained out of the turnover of final goods accrues to the entrepreneur. The share in income of each group is thereby determined by market forces. *Say's law*, the renowned theory of markets (*la théorie des débouchés*), sets out the argumentation for the corresponding share of income of each factor. The demand of consumers for final goods determines the entrepreneur's demand for input production factors. The price system balances out a possible surplus of either demand or supply.[16] Say even suggests a market for entrepreneurs: the demand in the goods market implies the demand for entrepreneurs. The supply of entrepreneurs is constrained by the individuals' personal and environmental context. A potential entrepreneur needs a sufficient amount of capital, either provided by others or by himself, to ensure his solvency. Moreover, a charismatic personality that foreshadows entrepreneurial success in order to use essential connexions and bear the burdens of an entrepreneurial life.[17]

A further important note concerning the distribution of income has to be made. The entrepreneur needs capital to finance the required productive factors in advance. The recompensation of them happens before possible revenues can be collected. Hence, the entrepreneur pays an ex ante negotiated remuneration to production factors and stays with the residual, *uncertain* income that remains from the revenues drawn off the turnover.

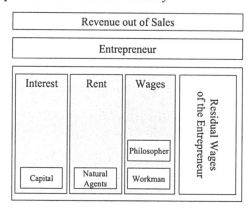

Figure 1.3: The income distribution of Jean-Baptiste Say's system.

1.3 The Classical School

According to Hébert and Link (1982)[18] the Classical School, all in all, neglected the entrepreneur and did not manage to develop an independent theory on entrepreneurship. Pre-classical as well as classical writers did not even use the term *entrepreneur*. When they touched entrepreneurial functions they used terms such as *adventurer, projector* or *undertaker*. **Adam Smith** (1723 – 1792) focused on capital as the decisive element in economic development. Parallel to Turgot, he saw the *undertaker, decision-maker* or *projector*, respectively, as a capitalist in the first place, and, moreover he reduced the entrepreneur to an ordinary economic agent that just puts his capital at stake. This is even more surprising given that Smith knew Quesnay and therefore was in touch with the French School.[19] **David Ricardo** (1772 – 1823) almost ignored the notion of an entrepreneurial element in his writings. A plausible explanation for this might be that Ricardo had a different understanding of what political economy was.[20] He regarded it as a science of laws where an entrepreneur could not fit in.[21] Other classical economists such as **John Stuart Mill** (1806 – 1873), and **Thomas R. Malthus** (1766 – 1834) are hardly cited in the context of entrepreneurship literature, nor did they contribute any major improvements to that theory,[22] even though Casson (1982) ascribes them a certain influence on the research of entrepreneurship.[23] **Alfred Marshall** (1842 – 1924) collected various ideas to entrepreneurship and labeled the entrepreneur a coordinator, superintendent, uncertainty-bearer. He discussed the entrepreneur's role but did not state the unique function of the entrepreneur.[24] The only writer who concentrated more on the entrepreneur than his classical contemporaries, was **Jeremy Bentham** (1748 – 1832). Bentham was a close follower of the French School. In contrast to Smith, who was his mentor, he conceptualized the entrepreneur in his work, although he never used the term entrepreneur but, corresponding to Smith, named him *projector*. Bentham fiercely criticized Adam Smith for the negative picture he painted of the *projector* as a wasteful, self-interest-driven man.[25] Bentham was quite far ahead of his time. He assigned the active role in economy to the creative entrepreneur, as Redlich (1949) interprets what Bentham termed the *projector*. He saw the projector as anything but an ordinary economic agent, and anticipated Schumpeter's heroic vision of the entrepreneur as an innovator.[26]

To sum up, although British classical economists touched the role of the entrepreneur in their writings, they did not explicitly develop a theory on entrepreneurship.

1.4 The German Classics and the German Historic School

Hébert and Link (1982) discuss the following German classical economists: **J. H. von Thünen** (1785 – 1850), **H. K. von Mangoldt** (1824 – 1858), **Gottlieb Hufeland** (1760 – 1817), **Friedrich Hermann** (1795 – 1868) and **Adolph Riedel** (1809 – 1872). The work of those economists is closely related to Say's *Treatise*,[27] which had been translated at the beginning of the 19th century. The concepts of Hufeland (1815) and Hermann (1832) were focused on income distribution, with the entrepreneur receiving remuneration for his special capabilities. Riedel (1838–43) linked his concept to Cantillon's, explaining the entrepreneur as an uncertainty reducer for other risk-averse economic actors; by doing this, he increases his own risk.[28] As already mentioned, most of their works underlined the entrepreneurial concept of the French School. The design of Thünen (1921) reminds us of Cantillon's production and distribution theory.[29] He subdivided the entrepreneurial income by subtracting wages of management and insurance against business losses from the *entrepreneur's residual wages* similar to the distribution theory of Say in figure 1.3. Thus, he specified the role of the entrepreneur in more detail. The entrepreneur might be but does not need to be the manager. Even though the manager may be equal to the entrepreneur in qualifications and capabilities, it is the entrepreneur who spends sleepless nights because of the risk he takes. This makes him more engaged and also innovative to ensure a successful business venture. Hence, the residual entrepreneurial income contains a recompensation for the risk he takes and it contains a *return to ingenuity*.[30]

The German Historic School was founded by **Wilhelm Georg F. Roscher** (1817 – 1894). In his *Die Grundlagen der Nationalökonomie*[31] he opened up a discussion of institutional aspects within economic theorizing.[32] To

Roscher, it was not enough to just look at the individual not taking into account the national differences in religion, science, language, art, law, etc. He gathered a lot of data adequate to describe the social and economic development of a nation and its population in order to derive general propositions. **Bruno Hildebrand** (1812 – 1878) and **Karl Knies** (1821 – 1898) followed Roscher on this path. It was **Gustav Schmoller** (1838-1917) within the German Historic School who discussed the entrepreneur. He analyzed a vast quantity of historic data and found a crucial element in economy which was the entrepreneur, an energetic, active man: a coordinator, manager and innovator. However, he did not enhance the theory of entrepreneurship.

The central point of interest within the German Historic School, however, was not the investigation of the entrepreneur.

Notes

[1] Compare Casson (1990).

[2] Hébert and Link (1982, p. 152).

[3] There were others before Cantillon who touched the entrepreneurial function in their work, but with regard to economic analysis Cantillon has to be seen as the precursor of the entrepreneur in economic theory. See Hébert and Link (1982) for further details.

[4] See Cantillon's work *Essai sur la nature du commerce en général*, Cantillon (1931). Already in his early times he covered a lot of the successive discussion on entrepreneurship. He made the entrepreneur the pivotal point of his theory.

[5] Compare Cantillon (1931).

[6] *Physiocracy* stands for the rule of nature.

[7] See Hébert and Link (1982, p. 31).

[8] See Hébert and Link (1982, p. 31).

[9] Compare Groenenwegen (1971).

[10] Compare Turgot (1977) and Hébert and Link (1982, p. 33).

[11] As figure 1.1 shows, Say is classified as a member of the French School, which, all in all, is quite a bold venture. His nationality would definitely not disapprove of it, whereas the fact that Say himself many times referred to Adam Smith and obviously highly valued Smith's *Wealth of Nations* would suggest a closer link to the Classics. See Say (1845) for a more profound inquiry. Some associate Say neoclassical economics (see e.g. Roll (1961). Others consider him a member of the Austrian School. His contributions to economic theory are huge so that different classifications are obviously possible. Nevertheless, Say's entrepreneurial concept is located closely to the French School.

[12] Compare Barreto (1989, p. 6).

[13] Say (1845, p. 20).

[14] Barreto (1989, p. 11).

[15] Hébert and Link (1982, p. 38).

[16] Compare Say (1845).

[17] For further details see Barreto (1989, p. 12).

[18] Hébert and Link (1982, chapter 5).

[19] Some economists are of a different opinion and say this interpretation to be derogatory. Pesciarelli (1986, p. 522) assures that "(...) the concept of the entrepreneur can indeed be found in the *Wealth of Nations*, and in at least three different forms. The first of these (also historically) is the figure of the adventurer. (...), and in Smith's [vocabulary] most frequently associated with the term merchant. It was also used to refer to entrepreneurial or speculative activities of various kinds." Redlich (1949) also constributes to this discussion. Nevertheless, it can be stated that Smith did not coin the theory on entrepreneurship.

[20] Cole (1946, p. 3) put the Ricardian treatment of the entrepreneur this way: "(...) not merely is the term itself absent in Ricardo's writings, but no concept of business leaders as agents of change (other than as shadowy bearers of technological improvements) is embraced in his treatment of economic principles."

[21] Hébert and Link (1982, p. 50).

[22] See Hébert and Link (1982, p. 54).

[23] See Casson (1982, p. 37) counts Mill (1848) among the ones who shaped the functional concept of the entrepreneur.

[24] Barreto (1989, p. 53) and Marshall (1948).

[25] Compare Pesciarelli (1986, p. 525).

[26] See Redlich (1949, p. 7).

[27] See Say (1845).

[28] Hébert and Link (1982, p. 56).

[29] See figure 1.3.

[30] See Hébert and Link (1982, p. 57).

[31] Roscher (1922).

[32] Compare Perlman and McCann (1998).

2 The Neoclassical Era

2.1 The Birth of Neoclassical Analysis

Chapter 1 gave us a lot of intuition on the subject matter. Economists put forward different aspects that have to be taken into account when investigating the entrepreneur. The emphasis was put on the entrepreneur's role as a coordinator, risk-taker, capitalist, etc. All in all, almost every writer recognizes the entrepreneur as a unique element in economic life.

Proceeding along the historical path of entrepreneurship research, we will see that basically the intuition has never vanished with regard to the important position of entrepreneurs in economy. Nevertheless – and that is why a cesura has to be made at a certain point in time – around the 1870s[1] a new era in economic thinking started, an era that created a masterpiece of a methodological toolbox apt to investigate economic phenomena in a stringent and consistent way. Those economists we nowadays call the founders of the Neoclassical School, such as Jevons, Walras and Menger. They had developed a standardizing body that seemed to enable us to handle the whole complexity of the economic world. The neoclassical methodology definitely was and still is an extraordinary accomplishment in economics. Undeniably, a lot of insights have ever since been gained in all respects of economic theorizing, but when we talk about entrepreneurial behavior, we encounter the boundaries of the neoclassical paradigm. When we question the role of the entrepreneur, we challenge methodology and this is why we have to trace back the path that led to an explanatory dead end in the research of entrepreneurship.

As already mentioned, the 1870s saw the beginning of the Neoclassical School. The publication of **Léon Walras** *Eléments d'économie pure*[2] can be seen as the first comprehensive synthesis of neoclassical thoughts which was the concept of general equilibrium.

William Stanley Jevons (1835 – 1882) enhanced the theory of Smith and Ricardo[3] and introduced marginal utility. **Carl Menger** (1841 – 1921) provided the mathematical toolkit for a corresponding analysis.[4] The way was smoothed to develop a theory of the firm that had to do without the entrepreneur. The following has been discussed extensively in literature, so that only a short summary of the disappearance of the entrepreneur in neoclassical theory need be given.[5] The neoclassical setting established at that time made possible to develop a modern production theory[6] which basically consists of three optimization problems: First, to find the minimal cost input mix; second, to produce the profit-maximizing output; and third, to employ inputs optimally. As it is well known by first-year economics students, the solutions of those three problems coincide when marginal revenues equal marginal cost. Thünen was the first to put forward a verbal formulation of this concept.[7] Wicksteed (1992) elaborated the graphical and mathematical formulation showing that each production factor receives its marginal revenue. Wicksell (1934) rounded off the optimization problem as he formalized the notion that when marginal revenues equal marginal cost the optimal quantity of input factors to be employed is reached. The optimization problem at the output side was already discussed in 1838 by Cournot (1927) which is also well-known in standard textbook economics. A lot of work had still to be done at that time: Marshall analyzed the upward-sloping supply curve.[8] Roy Harrod and Jacob Viner reflected on short-run cost curves.[9] The task to put the pieces together into a whole was spurred by Irving Fisher, solving the consumer's optimization problem.[10] The consumer maximizes utility by choosing to buy the optimal mix of goods subject to a budget constraint. It was obvious that consumers and producers faced the same optimization problem – at least from a mathematical point of view. The completion of the production theory was done by William Ernest Johnson when he set forth a verbal, mathematical and graphical representation of both the consumers' as well as producers' optimization problem. Figure 2.1 shows the graphical illustration.

Yet, a full integration of the different facets of the firm's optimization problem had not been accomplished. Léon Walras, Arthur L. Bowley and John R. Hicks tried what Joan Robinson finally managed to do: she showed that the firm's profit can either be investigated from the output side or from the factor market side.[11] Barreto (1989) names some of those economists[12] who contributed at the beginning of the 20th century to a full integration of a firm's optimization problems, connecting the factor market side to the output side and fitting the whole system into a general equilibrium framework. Paul Samuelson has become one of the best-known economists for those achievements.[13]

This is the path Barreto (1989) draws of the disappearance of the entrepreneur in microeconomic theory. Not only was the entrepreneur gradually

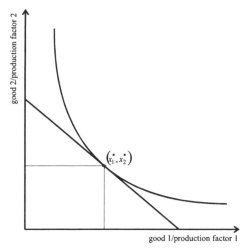

Figure 2.1: The graphical representation of the consumer's and producer's optimization problem.

Note: From the consumer's perspective we consider the budget constraint and the indifference curve, from the producer's perspective we deal with isoquants and isocost lines.

lost sight of, but the methodological framework that has been developed and widely accepted made it almost impossible to integrate the entrepreneur into an equilibrium system.

Let us briefly continue the walk along the neoclassical path. When we think of figure 2.1 as the representation of the firm's optimization problem, it is not hard to make a step further to the underlying production function. Figure 2.2 shows the corresponding three-dimensional homogeneous production function with diminishing returns to scale.

A cut, parallel to the K-L-plane,[14] results in a two-dimensional production function with one factor remaining constant and the other one being varied. That is what we call partial factor variation.

The theory of the firm assumes that a firm constantly produces on its production function (figure 2.2) at a given level of technology, which means that the firm produces efficiently. This implies that the firm minimizes costs (figure 2.1). Cost-minimization depends on the mix of input factors and their prices. Factor prices depend on their marginal product. The total demand for input factors is derived from the demand for output goods by consumers. Consumers' demand for output goods is determined by the utility consumers draw out of the consumption of those goods. The counterpart to the firm's production function is the consumer's utility function. In the same way the production function implies isoquants, the utility func-

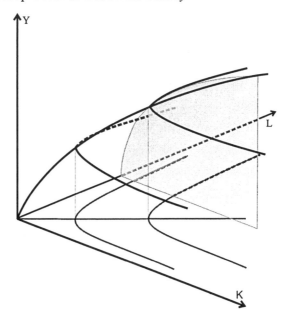

Figure 2.2: The neoclassical production function.

tion provides for indifference curves. Hence, we return to figure 2.1 which tells us exactly the consumer's optimality calculation for his optimal consumption pattern. The latter will be pointed out in figure 2.3. It will eventually show that in such a framework, the entrepreneur has to be neglected because there is no space left for him in such kind of approach.

The complete system

Figure 2.3 gives a simplified version of the general equilibrium framework. Suppose there are only consumers (households) and producers (firms). Households offer their labor on the factor market and demand consumer goods on the goods market. Producers demand labor on the factor market and, on the goods market, they sell the goods produced. This is the real part of the circular flow within economy. Correspondingly, the flow of money in the economy is as follows: producers pay wages to households and households, in return, pay the price for the goods they consume.

The first quadrant represents the goods market and the third quadrant the factor market.[15] The second quadrant shows the firms' aggregate production function, PF_0, we discussed above. The fourth quadrant maps the price system of the factor market and the goods market. At first, we look at the goods market. The indices of all parameters signify the initial state of

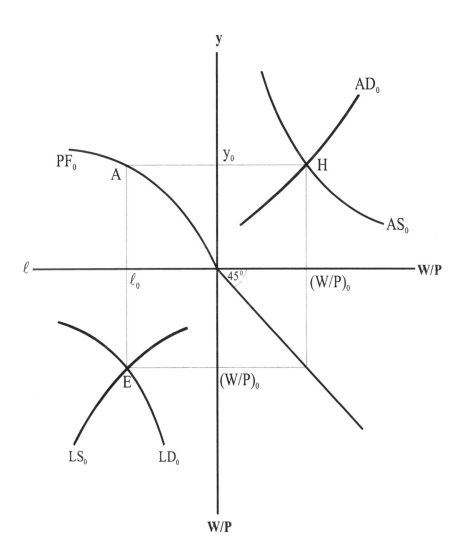

Figure 2.3: The general equilibrium system.

the system. The reason why aggregate demand, AD_0, portrays an upward-sloping curve is that the horizontal axis denotes real wages $\frac{W}{P}$. Wages are usually not discussed in the goods market. Therefore, let us set W equal to one. Price P is in the denominator, so that the usually downward sloping aggregate demand curve is flipped. Accordingly, the aggregate supply curve AS_0 is flipped, too. In H, the goods market is in equilibrium and total output Y_0 is determined. In the second quadrant, the corresponding point of production is shown in A, which delivers the amount of factor units l_0 employed, when C is produced efficiently at minimal costs. The labor market in the third quadrant – since there is only one factor of production – is equilibrated in E, where firms' aggregate labor demand LD_0[16] equals households' aggregate labor supply LS_0.[17] Thus, the level of nominal wages W is determined in the factor market and the price level P is determined in the goods sector; consequently, general equilibrium is reached in both markets at a given ratio $(\frac{W}{P})_0$. Since all agents, producers as well as households, exert optimal performance, a state of *Pareto-efficiency* has been reached. Hence, there is no incentive for any agent to change behavior; innovation, entrepreneurial behavior and structural change have no endogenous legitimation.

Ever since economists started to theorize on human behavior, they have been looking for consistency in theory. What classical theorists could not achieve, neoclassical economists succeeded in. The marginal school and, in particular, the Walrasian general equilibrium theory eliminated the shortcomings in terms of inconsistency within economic theory. They managed to refine the patchwork of classical thoughts to a consistent unity, but at the cost of some important aspects of the economic world. The ingenious accomplishments of Walras, Jevons, Menger and other contemporaries at that time had some side effects concerning the assumptions to be made in order to exert such kind of mathematical calculation. Those assumptions, listed below, require a certain type of an omnipotent economic agent, which was named *Homo economicus*:

i) *Each consumer's preferences are described by a utility function with positive first and negative second derivatives.*

ii) *Each producer's set of technical possibilities are described by a production function with positive first and negative second derivatives.*

iii) *Competitive behavior assumes that the quantities demanded and supplied will be equaled in every market, and that excessive profits will be eliminated.*

iv) *Marginal utility and marginal cost determine equilibrium in the market, and marginal productivity and marginal disutility determine equilibrium in the factor market.*

v) *There is perfect competition.*[18]

Economic agents and economic processes are represented by functions. The functions build a set of equations which results in an equilibrium point. In other words, if economic agents cannot be described by functions no equilibrium point can be calculated. The bottom line is: *equilibirium* requires *optimal behavior*, *optimal behavior* presumes *perfect rationality*, and finally, *perfect rationality* requires *perfect foresight* and *information*. In the following section the necessary set of assumptions will be sketched to show which implications the neoclassical methodology generated for economic analysis in general and for the entrepreneur specifically.

2.2 Searching for the Entrepreneur in Neoclassical Theory

Now, the question to be answered is where the entrepreneur could fit in. In section 1.1 we find the different connotations of the entrepreneur ever since the term was mentioned in literature by Hébert and Link (1982).[19] Yet, we cannot discuss all of the items discussed in chapter 1.1. But we can pick out the ones that fit into a general equilibrium framework in the following manner: item 2 (supplier of financial capital), 6 (manager or superintendent), 8 (owner of an enterprise) and 9 (employer of factors of production) suggest a picture of a static entrepreneur that does not take a key role in economic life, which most writers intuitively ascribed to him. As Hébert and Link (1982) put it: *"Only in a dynamic world does the entrepreneur become a robust figure."* The remaining eight items provide a dynamic notion of the entrepreneur. Even though it seems obvious that we cannot discuss dynamic aspects within a static model such as figure 2.3 yet it is the starting point to find out to what extent the idea of entrepreneurial behavior can be pursued with such a basic setting. Item 1 puts forward uncertainty and item 2 suggests that the entrepreneur is a decision maker. In a general equilibrium, we will always reach efficiency, i.e. a state of *(Pareto) optimality*. Consequently, this kind of entrepreneur will never make any wrong decisions, so that uncertainty cannot be the subject matter in his decision making process. Decision-making and therefore uncertainty can only be dominant features in disequilibrium. So are items 7 (the entrepreneur as organizer and coordinator of resources), 10 (the entrepreneur as contractor), 11 (the entrepreneur as allocator) and 12 (the entrepreneur as allocator of resources). This leaves us with items 3 and 5, the entrepreneur as in-novator and industrial leader, respectively. A static equilibrium does not allow for justifying a dynamic entrepreneurial figure that tries to change a state of optimality. Therefore, as figure 2.4 shows, economic change is banned to the outer economic sphere: in most equilibrium models, inno-vation is treated as an exogenous shock. Hence, the entrepreneur as an innovator and industrial leader must be an exogenous element, too.

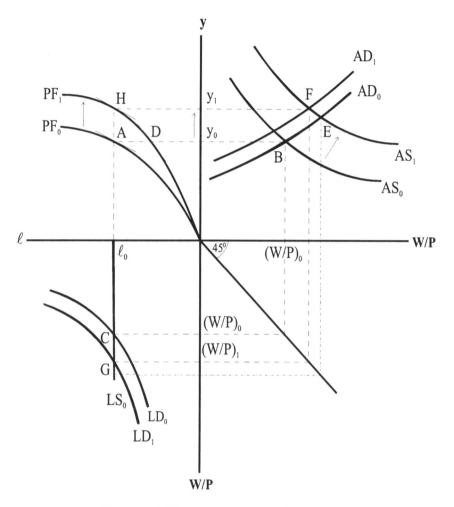

Figure 2.4: The comparative statics system.

For a graphic illustration within this framework (figure 2.4), suppose a positive exogenous shock occurs and the productivity is increased.[20] The production function in the second quadrant will shift up (proportionately) towards PF_1 inducing simultaneously a shift of the aggregate supply curve to AS_1, since every producer is willing to supply a higher quantity of output goods for a given price level $(\frac{W}{P})_0$. The shift of the aggregate supply curve causes an endogenous movement along the aggregate demand curve, AD_0, to point E. On the factor market, according to the standard textbook case, the workers' increased productivity, i.e. their marginal product, initiates a shift of the labor demand curve LD_0 to LD_1. Yet, general equilibrium has not readjusted. The shift of the aggregate supply curve, which led to the reputed equilibrium point E does not coincide with the real-wage ratio $(\frac{W}{P})_1$. In order to accomplish that, the aggregate demand curve must also shift to AD_1, which basically describes Say's renowned *law of markets*: *supply creates its demand*. Eventually, general equilibrium has been reached in points F, G and H. In short: to reach equilibrium after an increase in productivity, the labor demand curve as well as the aggregate supply curve have to shift; meaning one and the same thing, since labor demand depends on the firms' output level, the output level depends on aggregate demand, aggregate demand reflects households' preferences which implies households' labor supply. The conclusion is that the explanatory power of such an analytical system is confined to ends, not means. Although Walras himself emphasized the importance of entrepreneurs in real life, for analytical reasons he thought this would not be a necessary point for discussion. Walras starts where the economic function of an entrepreneur has already been performed efficiently.[21]

Figure 2.4 was an attempt to illustrate the bone of contention from a simple, static perspective. There are also a number of neoclassical models dealing with dynamics. Kihlstrom and Laffont (1979) develop a general equilibrium model. They manage to implement into an equilibrium model the decision process of economic agents whether they want to become an employee, and, therefore, earn less risky wages, or whether they want to become an entrepreneur and gain risky profits. Kihlstrom and Laffont instigate the process by implementing dynamic wage changes, whereby they start with comparative statics and continue with a dynamic analysis. They concede that their procedure is subject to the same criticism as the one we discussed above.[22] Justman (1996) also touched entrepreneurship and modelled *swarming mechanics* within a general equilibrium framework using a dynamic optimization technique to determine equilibrium. The calculation process is done backwards, starting form the distant future to determine optimal behavior.[23] Again, we see the symptomatic treatment of a dynamic element such as the entrepreneur within equilibrium. There are many equilibrium models that start out with a set of intuitive ideas which are pursued until the general equilibrium framework stipulates an optimizing, perfect rational economic agent deprived from the possibility of failure. Hence, the entrepreneur can neither be an innovator nor can he be a leader.

Technical change and innovation is exogenous; a need for a leader is absent in a system where all actors know their optimal paths.

Notes

[1] Compare Hébert and Link (1982, p. 63).

[2] The first edition appeared in 1874 and a revision of it was published in 1926. See Walras (1954).

[3] Smith and Ricardo differentiated utility and value. There is no inherent value to commodities or goods but the value is dependent, besides the scarcity of the good, on the utility one draws out of usage. See Ricardo (1821, ch. 1).

[4] For a detailed inquiry see Menger (1968). It has to be mentioned at this point that Menger did not only supply the proper mathematics but also founded a new school of thought which is known as the Austrian School. In his *Grundsätze* he discusses the concept of marginal utility and introduces the subjectivist view of individuals. For more information about the Austrian School, see chapter 3.

[5] Barreto (1989, p. 69) shows the whole process in detail.

[6] This is what we nowadays call standard textbook production theory. It can be found in any introductory textbook on microeconomics.

[7] Compare Thünen (1921).

[8] See Marshall (1948).

[9] Compare Harrod (1930) and Viner (1931).

[10] Compare Fisher (1925).

[11] Compare Robinson (1969, p. 251).

[12] Allen, Bowley, Coase, Frisch, Georgescu-Roegen, Harrod, Hicks, Hotelling, R. F. Kahn, Kaldor, Knight, Leontief, H. L. Moore, Robbins, Robinson, Schneider, H. Schultz, Schumpeter, Viner and Zassenhaus. Barreto (1989, p. 93).

[13] See Barreto (1989, p. 93).

[14] As in the standard textbook fashion, K stands for the input of capital and L stands for the input of labor.

[15] For simplicity, a static representation is chosen, where, on top of it, only one production factor (i.e. labor) is discussed.

[16] Labor demand derive directly from the demand for output goods.

[17] Labor supply derive from the households optimal mix of labor and leisure time that yields maximal utility.

[18] Keita (1992, p. 62).

[19] See citation on page 4.

[20] There is one remark to be made with respect to the labor supply curve. In figure 2.4 an inelastic labor supply curve is used. There are also other types of labor supply curves such as an elastic and a backward bending one; those options would change the point of

equilibrium but they would not change the propositions made concerning the deficiencies of general equilibrium analysis when analyzing the entrepreneur.

[21]Compare Hébert and Link (1982, p. 72).

[22]See Kihlstrom and Laffont (1979, p. 734).

[23]In this model he uses Bellman equations to analyze a single-firm's optimization behavior. Bellman equations facilitate a recursive optimization calculation, whereby several possible dynamic paths are determined and the expected value of the present value of each path is computed. Eventually, the optimal path is taken.

3 The Austrian School

Entrepreneurship research has been a focal point in Austrian economics. Paradoxically, the Austrian School put forth major achievements in neoclassical economics but also confronted neoclassical procedures with its deficiencies as discussed above. Due to its bifurcating position in economic analysis, the Austrian tradition is put third in this brief historical sketch.

3.1 Founders and Disciples

Carl Menger (1840 – 1921) marks the beginning of the Austrian School. At the same time that Jevons published his *Theory of Political Economy*,[1] Menger presented his *Principles*[2] in which he develops the Austrian theory of utility and value.

To his mind, there was no objective value of anything that exists per se. Neither it is scarcity of goods, nor resources. Value comes into existence after utility is incurred. Menger emphasized the consumer's side. The subjective value is derived from the utility the consumer can draw off consuming a certain good.[3] In contrast to this, the classical view of value and price was biased to the supply side: the *exchange* value of goods would be derived from the price which is determined by supply and demand, whereas supply is a function of production costs.[4] Only when "things" are useful or at least can be transformed into being useful "things" so that the consumer's needs can be satisfied, can a subjective value be determined. Menger emphasizes the role of human beings that strive to satisfy their needs and they only succeed when they undertake human action. To his mind, value depends on the following conditions:

1. *There must be a human need.*

2. *The "thing" that is to fulfill the need must possess properties that enable the individual to form a causal connection between that and satisfaction.*

3. *The individual must "know" of this connection.*

4. *The individual must be able to command access to the "thing" and be able to direct it to the satisfaction of the need.*[5]

Proceeding this way, the satisfaction of needs is not limited to a cognitive process of an individual but it also depends on environmental conditions. The individual has to consider the objective reality since:

> *All things are subject to the law of cause and effect. This great principle knows no exception, and we would search in vain in the realm of experience for an example to the contrary. Human progress has no tendency to cast it in doubt, but rather the effect of confirming it and of always further widening knowledge of the scope of its validity. Its continued and growing recognition is therefore closely linked to human progress.*[6]

The satisfaction of needs, therefore, has two determinants: one is internal to the individual and the other is the state of the external world. When the individual begins to understand the external determinants and its dependence on it, he is able to adjust his actions to satisfy his needs. By doing this, the external world is changed and this brings along further changes since the whole economic world underlies the law of cause and effect.[7]

Consequently, *human action* becomes the dynamic element in Austrian economics. The value of goods is the imputed potential of goods to satisfy needs: lower-order goods first have to be transformed into useful first-order (i.e. consumable) goods. Lower-order goods might be lower in value, they can even be of zero value taking into account that obviously useless goods are produced in economic reality. Value can be created provided that human *knowledge* enables economic agents to make the necessary causal links to produce valuable goods. Furthermore, the agent has to be entitled to exert necessary actions, which addresses the prerequisite of individuals' *property rights*.

The transformation process, according to Menger, is time-consuming. As the causalities might change in the course of time, this transformation process is *uncertain*. The producer requires, besides technological knowledge, *foresight* to meet future consumers' needs. Future wants are predictable – not perfectly, but at least to a certain degree – otherwise human action would not occur. Hence, *uncertainty* becomes the driving force of human action; whereas knowledge about markets and existing first-order goods is essential to forecast consumers' needs in order to plan and conduct an efficient production process.

The latter is exerted by an economizing individual: the entrepreneur. The entrepreneur basically has to predict consumers' future needs in order to produce a potentially useful good. Then, he has to acquire the necessary *technological knowledge* and the *knowledge* to select the adequate means from the ones available. Second, an *economic calculation* is vital to ensure efficient production to combine lower-order goods whose value is determined by the prospective value of the first-order good to be produced. Third, *the act of will* assigned to a human being (the entrepreneur) that initiates the igniting spark of any dynamic development.[8] Out of the latter two aspects it is clear that Menger's entrepreneur was a capitalist-entrepreneur.[9]

Eugen von Böhm-Bawerk (1851 – 1914) and **Friedrich Freiherr von Wieser** (1851 – 1926) were Menger's intellectual followers. Böhm-Bawerk put the bits and pieces together, not making essential contributions himself, to build the edifice of the Austrian School. Wieser worked on the subjectivist view of utility and especially emphasized property relations. The entrepreneur he described as a

> *(...) director by legal right and at the same time by virtue of his active participation in the economic management of his enterprise. He is a leader in his own right. He is the legal representative of the operation, the owner of the material productive goods, creditor for all accounts receivable and debtor for all accounts payable. As a lessor or lessee he is obligated or privileged. He is the employer under all contracts for work and labor ... His economic leadership commences with the establishment of the enterprise, he supplies not only the necessary capital but originates the idea, elaborates and puts into operation the plan, and engages collaborators. When the enterprise is established, he becomes its manager technically as well as commercially.*[10]

After World War I, **Ludwig Edler von Mises** (1881 – 1973) acceded Austrian economics. His objective was to pursue a deductive science to advance to the *truth*, independent of historical data but suitable to explain historic events. Mises objected to a radically positivistic view that empirical data alone has to be the platform gaining insights by induction, thus denying any rational, hypothetic-deductive approach.

He divides the universe into two parts: the realist part which eludes from a factual human understanding subject to epistemological reservations, and the rational part which is created by a cognitive process of human beings. The first part conceptualizes realism, affirming that there is a true reality independent of any cognitive representation. Hence, the deliberate conclusion would be empiricism, which contradicts such a rational component. Consequently, mankind is not able to access reality by rational, conclusive reasoning; any aprioristic theory has to be abandoned and any hypothetic-deductive methodology is useless. The second part of Mises' distinction – at first sight paradoxical – brings in rationality. The decisive difference, however, lies in Mises' concept of rationality. Neither does he claim that mankind would be able to perceive and understand reality in its nature nor that it is possible to make any a priori axiomatic assumptions. But economic behavior is aim-oriented and based on logical reasoning and in this sense human behavior is a priori rational.[11] Mises labels this concept the concept of *praxeology*,[12] *"(...)the aprioristic theory of human action."*[13] *Praxeology* was the axiomatic foundation he suggested for economic analysis. This concept has become Mises underpinning of the (Austrian-type) subjectivist view and in terms of methodology the call for methodological individualism. To his mind, economics had to be a science built on logic and mathematics but also to include institutional aspects.

Although this approach was in contradiction to a positivist and inductive view, Mises left room for an empiric investigation of such general laws derived in his methodology. Owing to the imponderability of economic reality he linked aprioristic theory to empirical validation:

> *Economics does not follow the procedure of logic and mathematics. It does not present an integrated system of pure aprioristic ratiocination severed from any reference to reality. In introducing assumptions into its reasoning, it satisfies itself that the treatment of the assumptions concerned can render useful services for the comprehension of reality.*[14]

With his praxeological concept Mises managed to escape the epistemological critique on economics. Sciences, especially natural sciences, try to know what reality is. The praxeological approach is one step less demanding. It does not discuss ontological questions but rather investigates human action and its context of occurrence, whereby human action is based on individuals' rational logic and their subjective perception of reality.

Mises originates from a quite philosophical stance and explores human action from a more realistic perspective, so he refrains from an optimizing economic agent and models an imperfect human being who acts according to his beliefs. Moreover, his notion of human action is a prerequisite for entrepreneurial behavior. His ideas about entrepreneurial behavior definitely are motivated by his praxeological conception, even though he has not developed an independent theory of entrepreneurship.

> *Economics, in speaking of entrepreneurs, has in view not men, but a definite function. This function is not the particular feature of a special group or class of men; it is inherent in every action and burdens every actor. In embodying this function in an imaginary figure, we resort to a methodological makeshift. The term entrepreneur as used by catallactic theory means: acting man exclusively seen from the aspect of the uncertainty inherent in every action. In using this term we must never forget that every action is embedded in the flux of time and therefore involves a speculation. The capitalists, the landowners, and the laborers are by necessity speculators. So is the consumer in providing for anticipated future needs. (...) In the context of economic theory the meaning of the terms concerned is this: Entrepreneur means acting man in regard to the changes occurring in the data of the market (...).*[15]

The American tradition   Among other American economists Hébert and Link (1982) mention Frederick B. Hawley (1843 – 1929), John Bates Clark (1847 – 1938), Herbert Davenport (1861 – 1931) and Frank Taussig (1859 – 1940), Amasa Walker (1799 – 1875), his son Francis Walker (1840 – 1897) and finally Frank Knight (1885 – 1972).[16] Basically, the American tradition in entrepreurship research is deeply rooted in the Austrian tradition. Amasa Walker contributed some more precise ideas to the distinction of the capitalist and the entrepreneur. His son, Francis Walker, refreshed ideas of the French tradition. Hawley reflected on uncertainty till Clark came up with the distinction between insurable and non-insurable risk foreshadowing Knight's work, which will be discussed below. Furthermore, Clark assigned the dynamic part within the economy to the entrepreneur, again, motivating Knight, on the one hand, and on the other, giving Schumpeter a cue to an equilibrium – destroying agent. Similarly, Herbert Davenport aligned his entrepreneur concept to the thoughts of the Austrian School. He tried to make the entrepreneur the core element of economic theory,[17] although he did not succeed completely in his venture. A contemporary of Davenport, Frank Taussig, touched the innovative role of the entrepreneur in economy, while Schumpeter had already finished his seminal work on the *Theory of Economic Development*. Frank Knight was one

of the American economists who contributed most to the theory of entrepreneurship, as it is portrayed in the following section.

3.2 Knight and the Entrepreneur as Uncertainty Bearer

Frank Knight (1885 – 1972) resumed the topic of uncertainty what had
been put aside in a rather methodologically motivated discussion such as
Schumpeter's and Kirzner's.[18] After Cantillon had implicated uncertainty
in entrepreneurial behavior at the beginning of the 18th century, it had to
wait till 1921 when Knight published his work on *Risk, Uncertainty and
Profit*.[19] Knight discussed the importance of uncertainty in detail. He
distinguished *true uncertainty* from *risk*, the latter being insurable because
it can be parameterized by the probabilities of possible outcomes, whereas
the former type of uncertainty is uninsurable since neither the outcome nor
probabilities can be attached.

His criticism of *perfect knowledge* reflects the starting point of his entrepreneurial concept. Without uncertainty, the economic outcome would
simply be the result of a purely mechanistic process. Economic actors
would not differ in terms of their individual knowledge and their intellectual capacity. According to Knight, uncertainty is an economy-wide
feature affecting all economic agents, since economic actors are heterogeneous in their individual intellectual endowment. With perfect knowledge
missing, the economic actors have to make decisions on "what to do and
how to do it",[20] thus the pure act of exerting economic actions, once a decision is made, becomes less important in economic behavior. The way
agents deal with uncertainty induces heterogeneous economic behavior:

1. *an adaptation of men to occupations on the basis of kind
   of knowledge and judgment;*
2. *a similar selection on the basis of degree of foresight, for
   some lines of activity call for this endowment in a very
   different degree from others;*
3. *a specialization within productive groups, the individuals with superior managerial ability (foresight and capacity of ruling others) being placed in control of the
   group and the others working under their direction; and*
4. *those with confidence in their judgment and disposition
   to "back it up" in action specialize in risk-taking.*[21]

Based on these four points, Knight derives his concept of the entrepreneur, which he referred to as the *business man*:

> *Under the enterprise system, a special social class, the busi-*
> *ness men, direct economic activity; they are in the strict sense*
> *the producers, while the great mass of the population merely*
> *furnish them with productive services, placing their persons*
> *and their property at the disposal of this class; the entrepre-*
> *neurs also guarantee to those who furnish productive services*
> *a fixed remuneration.*[22]

Producers have to make predictions concerning the consumers' needs and accordingly, they have to coordinate production factors to produce tradable goods. That is, what Knight calls a situation of *uncertainty*. Only a small group of agents is willing to face uncertainty and, at the same time, has the *intellectual capacity* and *power* to *direct* and *control* others who are rather *doubtful* and *timid*. The latter have their *risk insured* by the former, that means, the entrepreneurs guarantee their employees a fixed income whereas the entrepreneurs bear the imponderableness of an uncertain future.[23]

3.3 Kirzner and the Entrepreneur as Arbitrageur

Israel M. Kirzner (born in 1930) also developed a comprehensive theory of the entrepreneur embedded in the realm of the Austrian School. Menger and Mises (his academic father), Böhm-Bawerk, Hayek among others delivered the preliminary Austrian-type framework Kirzner could build his entrepreneurial concept on. In his works *Competition and Entrepreneurship*[24] and *Perception, Opportunity and Profit*,[25] the role of Kirzner's entrepreneur in economy can be extracted.

Equivalently to the Austrian tradition he rejected the idea of simply exploring general equilibrium and its conditions, although he flirted with the idea of general equilibrium as we will see later on when talking about Kirzner's entrepreneur as an equilibrator. It would neglect important aspects in the economic system which not least enables the justification of any entrepreneurial element. Equilibrium denies the existence of markets because such a state of optimality does not allow for a lack of knowledge and capabilities of any agent involved, consumers as well as producers. Without such deficiencies of actors we end up in the tautological conclusion that there is no entrepreneur with superior knowledge if there is no agent with imperfect knowledge. If we allow for differences in knowledge on either side, consumers and producers (suppliers), we also allow for the discussion of markets and therefore talk about a situation of disequilibrium characterized by continuous change.[26] Kirzner refers to Hayek when talking about the role of markets to emphasize their importance of information diffusion in order to explain the entrepreneurial function:

> *Hayek's pioneering view of market process as being one of information dissemination and discovery (...) has given us: the guidepost to an entrepreneurial perspective on market processes.*[27]

Kirzner starts at the individuals' level. He presupposes a decision-making process which aligns with the Mengerian subjectivist valuation of individuals. They strive to fulfill their needs and act in a specific way, if they know how to make the causal connections and if they know how to make a "thing" to satisfy their needs. Hence, knowledge is the focal point of his entrepreneurship discussion.

Moreover, he narrows down the Misesian proposition of the entrepreneurial quality to be attached to each individual but he parallels the function of the individuals decision-making process to the function of the entrepreneur in the market. Human action is Mises' praxeological explanation for an individual's decision-making process basically saying that every economic actor is an entrepreneur, But, to Kirzner, as entrepreneurship refers to market interaction, this economic function of the entrepreneur is restricted to an individual *"(...) who buys in one market in order to resell, possibly at a considerably later date, in a second market."*[28] Overall, Kirzner's intention is to isolate the entrepreneurial element from any other economic function. A further step was to face the entrepreneur with the Robbinsian economizer who is an optimizer and therefore invulnerable to imperfections saying that he owns perfect knowledge about given means and ends, not making any mistakes and consequently, always hitting his target. It is obvious that this is not the type of man Kirzner has in mind.

He searches the entrepreneurial element in a Crusoe situation. The key to his approach is *spontaneous learning.*[29] Spontaneous learning suggests that there is a piece of knowledge Crusoe is not yet aware of. That is what Kirzner calls a *hunch*. The bits of information Crusoe consciously knows represent a pure resource he employs in production. *"But concerning Crusoe's hunches and his visions in the face of a changing, uncertain environment, it cannot be said at all that Crusoe knows he has a hunch or a vision of the future."*[30] It is not that all of a sudden Crusoe would know how to put his hunch into practice. *"He does not act by deliberately utilizing his hunch about the future; instead, he finds that his actions reflect his hunches."*[31] To conclude to the actual entrepreneurial element, it becomes obvious that *"(...) the essence of entrepreneurial vision, and what sets it apart from knowledge as a resource, is reflected in Crusoe's lack of self-consciousness concerning it. Crusoe does not 'know' that he possesses a particular vision, (...).*"[32] Subsequently, as he gradually realizes through the ends of his actions that his hunch was right towards a hoped result, the hunch becomes knowledge and the entrepreneurial vision vanishes. This process is a subconscious learning process, the recognition of a yet unrecognized entrepreneurial vision.

Spontaneous learning refers to all economic actors, consumers and producers. To Kirzner, the state of mind that nurtures the possibility to spontaneous learning is *alertness*. Every economic actor makes decisions, even if they do not have any resources, including *knowledge*. Nonetheless, decisions are made best to the individual's knowledge. He might recognize that he lacks some knowledge necessary to make the "right" decision, he might even be able to collect this kind of knowledge but this is not what denotes spontaneous learning in Kirzner's sense. Spontaneous learning can only occur with regard to knowledge which is, at the most, subconsciously known by the individual. It is a hunch, an intuition about the future which is spontaneously discovered and transformed into conscious knowledge. Then, the hunch has become a resource of production.

The consumer might learn spontaneously about new opportunities to satisfy his needs, he is alert to new means to satisfy his ends. The individual who is alert to market opportunities to make profits, Kirzner calls the entrepreneur.[33] This finally implies the act of will to complete entrepreneurial actions. The propensity to entrepreneurial behavior is increased if the alert individual believes that the accidentally discovered information is beneficial.[34]

Alertness is also the crucial quality that differentiates the Robbinsian economizer from the entrepreneur. Once the alert individual discovers, i.e. spontaneously acquires new knowledge, he is a pure entrepreneur. Then, knowledge has become conscious to the entrepreneur and therefore does not need further alertness and spontaneous learning to be used repetitively. Consequently, the entrepreneurial quality disappears and, if this individual lacks any other hunches, he becomes an ordinary Robbinsian economizer.

For analytical convenience, and as Kirzner wants to isolate the entrepreneurial element, he distinguishes between the *pure Robbinsian economizer* and the *pure entrepreneur*.

As mentioned above, Kirzner works out Ludwig von Mises' concept of *human action*. Individuals act on their subjective view of the economic situation. A common term for such sort of subjectivism is expectations. Not knowing the true situation, they have to make decisions based on their knowledge, which includes expectations about other actors and their environment; an individual's mental construct, mental connections built on perception and accumulated experience. Obviously, actors make mistakes and adjust their behavior to a changing environment; they learn from their mistakes. The adjustment process of their expectations is a subconscious one because no one is able to deliberately discover other persons' plans. The pure entrepreneur discovers subconsciously what he considers to be market opportunities to make future profits. Subsequently, he acts according to his hunch and seeks a capitalist to borrow money from in order to finance his venture. The production process has to be organized and launched to earn revenues to recompense production factors to remain with the residual, the entrepreneur's profit.

According to Kirzner, it has to be emphasized that the *pure* entrepreneur is neither a capitalist nor a coordinator of production factors. The only characteristic feature a pure entrepreneur owns is the role of an *arbitrageur*.[35]

The idea of Kirzner's entrepreneur is rooted in the Austrian tradition, the critique on equilibrium analysis. He also refrains from such theoretic conception while he assigns to the entrepreneur the role of an equilibrator. Human decision making and spontaneous learning operate equilibrating on the individuals as well as on the market level. In a world of uncertainty individuals become aware of available opportunities, and adequate actions are taken to increase their well-being. On the market level, entrepreneurs recognize opportunities and rearrange resource allocation. Hence, on the individuals' as well as the market level, mis-allocation and error are gradually eliminated.[36]

3.4 Schumpeter and the Entrepreneur as an Innovator

Schumpeter's methodology   The most popular view of the entrepreneur in economics has been developed by Joseph A. Schumpeter (1883 – 1950). His achievements in supporting a heterodox approach in economics had been so well received among economists that a whole strand of literature relates to him. Schumpeterian economics has become synonymous to innovation economics and economics of (technological) change. The key to his theoretical system is innovation and the element in this system to bring along innovation is the entrepreneur. His work is an allusion to the fundamental reservations of orthodoxy, though at his time, it was neglected for a long time. It is not that Schumpeter's thoughts were completely new, but he managed to collect numerous ideas to create a seminal platform for an alternative approach to economic analysis.

Schumpeter's work was tremendously influenced by a critical review on equilibrium theory. Though fascinated by Walras' system of equilibrium,

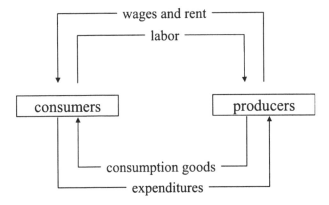

Figure 3.1: The circular flow.

he stated that equilibrium theory contributed as much as it could; but further insights could not be expected. Surely, Walras was not the only one who influenced Schumpeter's thinking. There are many others that delivered preparatory work affecting his *Theory of Economic Development* (first published in 1911), *Business Cycles* (1939) and later *Capitalism, Socialism and Democracy* (1942).

A closer look at his work shows roots in the edifice of thought of Weber, Menger, Wieser, Say, Hayek, Böhm-Bawerk, to name a few. Schumpeter is to be classified as an Austrian economist. Though fascinated by Say's work, where we evidently can find a lot of parallels to his formulation of the innovation process, and also his esteem of Walras, who probably was the source of his critique on the *circular flow*, Schumpeter processed mostly Austrian ideas.[37]

Quesnay developed the idea of the *circular flow* as an analogy to circulation of blood in humans.[38] Walras equilibrium system became the neoclassical formal representation of the circular flow. Schumpeter starts his critique right at that point. The circular flow is shown in figure 3.1:[39]

Schumpeter considered the circular flow as a static representation of an economic system. Consumers (or households) offer their labor and earn wages which they spend in return on consumption goods they buy from producers. Suppose we have one single agent in an economy, which means to say the agent lives in autarchy. Furthermore, we assume that the only thing he produces is pastry and consequently, as he is the only one within the system, eats it. The agent is consumer and producer in one person. Thinking in the way of the circular flow, he offers his labor force to the producer and produces five pieces of pastry. In return he gets paid the wages equivalent to five pieces of pastry. Being at the same time the consumer, he spends the money earned on consumption goods and buys five pieces of pastry as pastry is the only good he can buy. The circular flow is completed and thus the system is in equilibrium.[40] Yet, the thought of equilibrium in this context is intuitively obvious. When we expand the model to a system of two agents, one consumer and one producer, we simply split economic functions on two distinct agents. The gist of the train of thought remains the same, besides a necessary discussion, which will not be led here, about the distribution of productive factors and property rights among those two individuals. The equilibrium concept would suggest that the consumer in the same manner would offer his labor force, earn money, which he eventually would spend on consumption goods. But the decisive difference to the fictitious one-man economy is that the decision which quantity to produce and which quantity to consume fall apart and two independent agents make decisions based on the expected action of the other. Of course, it is still very easy for the producer to get to know how much the consumer wants to consume by simply asking him demanding in return the consumer's labor force. But as soon as we introduce a multitude of consumers and producers, the coordination process of each actor's plan to match the other actors' ones, the henceforth created complexity sheds doubts on the actual existence of an equilibrium. Knowledge, information and communication matter. Schumpeter calls such an equilibrium, if ever reached, a *timeless* and *static* system. All actors' plans have to coincide. From a theoretical perspective this is made possible by the definition of an equilibrium that implies optimal behavior according to perfect rationality.[41] This makes change impossible since the coincidence of all plans also includes the correct expectations on actors' future behavior. Hence, there cannot be an economic development.

The dynamic version of the circular flow also shows the *static* properties Schumpeter assigns to equilibrium analysis.[42]

Schumpeter advocates a dynamic system, a system subject to endogenous change. He understands the production process as a combination of production factors and he states the fact that there are changes in the way combinations are made. The occurrence of *new combinations* brings along change and disturbs the previously existing equilibrium.

> *It is spontaneous and discontinuous change in the channels of the flow, disturbance of equilibrium, which forever alters and displaces the equilibrium state previously existing. Our theory of development is nothing but a treatment of this phenomenon and the processes incident to it.*[43]

Schumpeter distinguishes five cases of new combinations, which he also calls innovations. They are:

(1) *The introduction of a new product or a new product quality.*

(2) *The introduction of a new production method.*

(3) *The opening of a new market.*

(4) *The use of new raw materials or sources of semimanufactures.*

(5) *The creation of a new industry organization.*[44]

These innovations do not fall from heaven but are initiated by economic actors, which Schumpeter calls the *entrepreneurs*.[45] The entrepreneur consequently is a disturber of equilibrium; he causes what Schumpeter named *creative destruction*, a term that has become the emblem of Schumpeterian research.

The innovation process after Schumpeter in figure 3.2 shows both Schumpeter's parallels to Say's production theory[46] and a methodological connotation of the creative destruction of a Walrasian static equilibrium.

Figure 3.2: The innovation process in Schumpeter's theory.

Thus, the entrepreneur becomes the core element of Schumpeter's dynamics of economic change. The creation of knowledge, to draw Schumpeter's parallels to Say, is accomplished by a *philosopher*. *Workers* execute the production process, which is the combination of *natural agents* and *capital*. The entrepreneur in Say's world takes the role of coordinating the entire production process. Schumpeter, however, discounted this function as the task of a pure manager but not of an entrepreneur. The entrepreneur is the one who carries out *new combinations*, he innovates. Other economic agents follow along the lines of the innovator, when they observe the successful diffusion process on the market side, and imitate the entrepreneur's actions. This way, *swarms of innovations* occur which lead to a boom till the economic system falls into recession inducing business cycles in the economic evolution.[47]

The qualities of Schumpeter's entrepreneur: in conclusion to Schumpeter's approach, the entrepreneur cannot be an optimally acting agent by definition. He destroys equilibrium, a superior, general state of optimality.

Moreover, all non-entrepreneurs cannot be of the kind of an *Homo economicus* either, a perfect rational economic actor. This would not allow for entrepreneurial behavior.

Schumpeter's methodological approach to the entrepreneur clearly advocates the necessity of a dynamic element in a de facto continuously changing economy. Equally, it is plausible to attribute such an element to a certain type of actor in economy. Without economic actors there is no economic world. Unfortunately, Schumpeter offered only a descriptive and intangible version of his entrepreneur, which is still difficult to detect in economy.

In summary, Schumpeter's entrepreneur was developed straight out of his reflections on economic change. The entrepreneur symbolized the dynamic element in economy. The entrepreneur was a *leader*. There might be many who know about economic opportunities but there are only few who are willing to *do the thing*, some who show leadership[48] and carry out *new combinations*. *"It is therefore, more by will than by intellect that the leaders fulfil their function, more by 'authority,' 'personal weight,' and so forth than by original ideas."*[49] He is someone special who has the ability and the strength to break through traditional structures and challenge the accepted way of doing things. Schumpeter's heroic entrepreneur thus parallels what Weber described a *charismatic leader*.[50] The entrepreneur is neither an economic man who simply weighs marginal cost and benefits to perform efficiently, nor a pure hedonist; he rather has

> *(...) the dream and the will to found a private kingdom, usually, though not necessarily, also a dynasty. (...) Then there is the will to conquer: the impulse to fight, to prove oneself superior to others, to succeed for the sake, not of the fruits of success, but of success itself. (...) Finally, there is the joy of creating, of getting things done, or simply of exercising one's energy and ingenuity.*[51]

Schumpeter clearly criticizes the concept of a *Homo economicus* and asks for an altered methodological approach to substantiate the entrepreneur.

Notes

1 Compare Jevons (1871).

2 Compare Menger (1968).

[3] From a philosophical perspective, this introduces constructivism into economic theory.

[4] In order this proposition to hold, a true objective value of resources has to exist.

[5] Menger (1968, p. 53).

[6] Menger (1968, p. 51).

[7] Menger opposed the radical empiristic procedure of the German Historical School, which denied any economic law to be deducible by pure analytical reasoning so that the last resort has to be "looking at the data" and by means of induction develop a comprehensive theory of economic phenomena in historic time (this describes the so-called "Methodenstreit" in those days). Menger made a step towards a "rational" world saying that there has to be some general laws because everything "(...) is subject to the law of cause and effect" (Menger (1968, p. 51)). This has become a paradigmatic assumption of the Austrian School. Human action only makes sense if there are causal links in economy. This has become known as the *praxeological* approach coined by Ludwig von Mises. Selgin (2001, p. 21) puts forward: "Praxeology represents an attempt to escape the nihilistic implications of both historicism and empiricism. It affirms the operation of inviolable laws within the realm of human action. It purports to establish the universal validity of these laws by deducing them from the allegedly incontestable truth that people act purposefully, the *axiom of action*."

[8] See Menger (1968), Perlman and McCann (1998, p. 420).

[9] Hébert and Link (1982) come to an opposite interpretation of Menger's entrepreneur.

[10] Wieser (1927, p. 324).

[11] See Kastrop (1993, p. 196).

[12] By and large, praxeology comes close to the Cartesian rationale: "*I think, therefore I am, was so certain and so evident that all the most extravagant suppositions of the sceptics were not capable of shaking it (...)*", (Descartes (1637, p. 53)).

[13] von Mises (1962, p. 73).

[14] von Mises (1959, p. 66).

[15] von Mises (1959, pp. 252–254).

[16] Compare Hébert and Link (1982, p. 84).

[17] See Davenport (1914).

[18] To be discussed later in this section.

[19] See Knight (1921).

[20] Knight (1921, p. 268).

[21] Knight (1921, p. 269).

[22] See Knight (1921, p. 271).

[23] Compare Knight (1921).

[24] Compare Kirzner (1973).

[25] Compare Kirzner (1999).

[26] See Kirzner (1973, p. 6).

[27] Kirzner (1999, p. 33).

[28] Kirzner (1999, p. 172).

[29] Kirzner (1999, p. 146).

[30] Kirzner (1999, p. 169).

[31] Kirzner (1999, p. 169).

[32] Kirzner (1999, p. 169).

[33] See Kirzner (1999, p. 130).

[34] See Kirzner (1999, p. 149).

[35] Kirzner (1973, p. 48).

[36] See Kirzner (1999, p. 171).

[37] Kirzner (1990).

[38] See previous section.

[39] Figure 3.1 has become a standard textbook diagram. See e.g Barreto (1989, p. 25).

[40] This illustrates also Menger's concept of subjective value, Mises implicit idea of "human action" and Kirzner's idea that an individual's human action is equilibrating. The individual draws utility from the consumption of pastry; that is, he is not hungry anymore. This attaches a subjective value to a piece of pastry. Since there are no other consumers there is no market and therefore there is no need for money and prices do not exist. The consumer has a need, knows the "thing" that satisfies this need, he has the knowledge how to produce this "thing", he is willing to act and he, last but not least, has the required property rights. Finally as his needs are satisfied, the individual is in equilibrium.

[41] Schumpeter (1934, chap. 1).

[42] Barreto (1989, p. 26).

[43] Schumpeter (1934, p. 64).

[44] Schumpeter (1934, p. 66).

[45] Schumpeter (1934, p. 75).

[46] Compare with figure 2.1.

[47] Schumpeter (1939a).

[48] Compare also Schumpeter (1939b, pp. 102).

[49] Schumpeter (1934, p. 88).

[50] See Weber (1965) in detail.

[51] Schumpeter (1934, p. 93).

4 Synthesis and Summary

In this part, a threefold analysis of the existing literature on entrepreneurship has been undertaken.

Chapter 1   sketches the multitude of ideas from the early 18th century to the 1870s. It exposes the roots of entrepreneurship research as well as attempts a categorization of strands of thoughts. The beginning was set with Cantillon[1] who had provided a basic scaffolding to be expanded by his successors: Quesnay incorporated the role of capital which was elaborated further by Turgot. Baudeau added innovation. Say rounded off the French School contributing not only to a distinct theory of the entrepreneur in economy but, moreover, delivered a platform for upcoming economists to shape a clear-cut, consistent and stringent theory of economics.

Classical economists were put aside a bit. This should not reduce the seminal insights they generated in economics but in terms of the theoretical treatment of the entrepreneur most had already been discussed by the French tradition.

The German Classics and the German Historic School also touched the topic of the entrepreneur, whereas the latter rather stirred up the *Methodenstreit* than focused on the entrepreneur.

Chapter 2   shows the advent of the Neoclassical era, when we experienced a unique convergence in economic thinking which has led to what we nowadays call standard textbook economics. It has more and more submitted itself to a compelling, mathematical elegance and a convincing methodology. But, as a by-product, the entrepreneur had to be sacrificed.

Chapter 3   contains heterodox approaches which are associated with the Austrian School, if such kind of distinction is legitimate at all.[2] Menger,

Mises, Böhm-Bawerk, Hayek, among others, refined the critique upon the neoclassical paradigm and, thus, supplied the foundation for other economists to build their theoretical framework on, which emphasized the importance of entrepreneurs in economy. Davenport, an American (Austrian-type) economist, even tried to make economics a theory of entrepreneurship.

The most promising and comprehensive concepts of the entrepreneur were picked out and shown in detail: most notably, Schumpeter and Kirzner but also Knight, developed explicit theories of entrepreneurship. They all started from the critique on orthodox theory emphasizing different aspects: Kirzner stressed the market process and alertness, Knight focused on uncertainty and knowledge, Schumpeter discussed economic change, innovation and, in particular, methodology. Knight made uncertainty the pivot of entrepreneurship. Concerning Schumpeter and Kirzner, there is a long-lasting debate about what the significant difference between these two concepts is, as Schumpeter's and Kirzner's entrepreneurs seem to look alike. Kirzner (1999) himself undertook the venture to clarify this distinction. He asserts that the *psychological profile* of Schumpeter's entrepreneur is valid and so is the idea of the entrepreneur as a *creative destructor*. But the entrepreneurial function in the real economic world is being alert to market opportunities. A personal psychological profile might be helpful for entrepreneurial actions; furthermore, entrepreneurial actions might be disruptive to existing structures. But only if an economic actor *passively* learns about an opportunity, only if he is alert, can he unfold his qualities of leadership and bring along the destruction of existing structures. To Kirzner, such a pre-existing structure cannot be a state of equilibrium; since any innovation creates a state of higher efficiency compared to the one before. By definition, equilibrium is a state of efficiency and a state preceding a state of "higher efficiency"[3]; therefore it cannot be a state of equilibrium.[4] Let the reader's taste make the decision whether this distinction between an equilibrium-disturbing and an equilibrium-creating entrepreneur provides further insights into entrepreneurship.[5]

Much more importantly, the Schumpeter–Kirzner discussion addresses methodology. Besides the intuition about entrepreneurship which had already been articulated by the French tradition and even mentioned in neoclassical theories,[6] theoretical work always comes to a halt at methodological issues. The question is which methodological approach to choose in order to gain further insights in entrepreneurship research. The dominant paradigm is the neoclassical methodology; but as we saw, there are two extreme views on that, the one saying that equilibrium theory does not allow for entrepreneurs, the other saying that entrepreneurs do not allow for equilibrium. The first basically reflects the symptomatic nihilism of neoclassical methodology towards the entrepreneur. The second reflects

Schumpeter's vision of the entrepreneur as an innovator, which suggests a heterodox approach to certain phenomena such as entrepreneurship and therefore does not allow equilibrium analysis. Kirzner tries to reconcile these two extreme views by taking into account the critique on neoclassical methodology.

Concerning the intention to investigate the entrepreneur the first option of methodology, which is equilibrium analysis, turns out to be inadequate, since the entrepreneur is believed to be an important figure in economy and therefore should also be an important figure in economics. Kirzner's intermediate position suggests disequilibrium analysis, whereby he primarily focuses on the market process rather than discussing methodology beyond the Austrian background he refers to. Schumpeter advocates and explicitly searches for a heterodox methodology and this makes him a prominent figure in heterodox economics. He showed that to investigate the entrepreneur means also to investigate methodology. He portrayed the interdependence between assumptions, modelling and methodology exemplifying the entrepreneur. Methodology is essential to model economic phenomena and modelling requires assumptions upon real-world phenomena. When we reject a model we might be able to retain a model's explanatory power by rearranging the underlying assumptions. In case, however, such rearrangements impinge on methodological constraints, we additionally have to question methodology. The Schumpeterian entrepreneur embodies the question of methodology. Unfortunately, Schumpeter did not couch in terms how such methodology looks like. Nonetheless, Schumpeter was one of the first to give guidance towards evolutionary economics.

In the next chapter a metatheoretical reflection is undertaken to find out fundamental aspects of a heterodox approach that allows to investigate entrepreneurial behavior.

Notes

[1] To set the beginning with Cantillon is common in economic literature, as he obviously introduced the entrepreneur to economics. With respect to the intellectual roots of entrepreneurship, it seems to be arbitrary, since many others before Cantillon, such as philosophers, dealt with such sort of phenomenon. Nevertheless, for the sake of this economic analysis it suffices to start at that point of history.

[2] Doing this, it has also become more difficult to sustain a distinct classification of economic schools of thought. The French School, the Classical School and the Austrian School contributed to neoclassical theory. The confusing part of the story might be, for example, Carl Menger, who is called the founder of the Austrian School, on the one hand, and, on the other, he is also one of the designated fathers of the Neoclassical School. Besides, the American tradition is strongly aligned to the Austrian tradition. There are further examples that seem to contradict to such classification of economic schools as it is undertaken in figure 1.1. For a better understanding, however, it appears to be profitable.

[3]The term "higher efficiency" is put in quotation marks because by nature the definition of efficiency there is no comparative. This leads us to the discussion of *static* and *dynamic* efficiency which will not be led in this context.

[4]Kirzner (1999).

[5]As a matter of perspective, if we allow to think of the alertness to market opportunities and the agent's implied human action as being a part of innovativeness – neglecting the question whether a state of equilibrium in a dynamic economic world will ever be reached before another dynamic entrepreneur comes along to prevent economy from equilibrium – it would leave us with the center-piece of the Schumpeterian dynamics of economic change, i.e. the entrepreneur.

[6]Walras, for example, also emphasized the importance of the entrepreneur in real economy but he suggested, for intellectual reasons, that it would be legitimate to start right after all adjustment processes which eventually lead to equilibrium, which means that all entrepreneurial actions have already been completed. Compare e.g. Bürgermeister (1994).

Part II

From the Evolution of Economics to the Economics of Evolution

5 Evolutionary Economics

5.1 Introduction

Part I illustrated both the intuition on entrepreneurial behavior as well as the overwhelming influence of methodology on economic thinking. The role of entrepreneurs in economy has always been recognized among economists. Nevertheless, in economic theory, the entrepreneur has gradually been buried in oblivion during the accession of a more and more dominant neoclassical paradigm. It is not surprising that neoclassical theory has become the paradigm of orthodox economics, as it is hard to escape the fascination of its clear-cut methodology, a methodology that renders invulnerable consistency by means of its mathematical formulation. The elegance of its formal treatment and the rigor in its reasoning elucidates tremendously the complexity of economic phenomena – and also offers the unambiguity of a deterministic world. The concessions to be made show up in the set of assumptions required by neoclassical methodology, concessions at the cost of the entrepreneur. The postulate of perfect rationality, including complete information and foresight, thereby is the most doubtful core assumption in such a framework.[1] Contrarily, if we relax the assumption of perfect rationality, we move towards a non-teleological framework, a world of arbitrariness, which seems to disallow any general propositions about economic behavior. The challenging venture to face such neoclassical shortcomings led to a movement amongst economists, which has become known as evolutionary economics.[2] To develop a possible evolutionary setting, the next section on the philosophy of science will sketch both the evolution of economic theory and the corollary of evolutionary theory as its necessary and logical endorsement, contrasting the neoclassical paradigm, in order to overcome some neoclassical shortcomings.

5.2 Economics and Philosophy of Science – Parallels and Prospects

Economics has its origin in philosophy and, in its nature, still is philosophy[3]; and as much as philosophy has been searching for a better understanding of mankind in general, economics has been trying to investigate the human being in his economic environment, and how he manages to cope with scarce resources and uncertainty. The path of philosophy was influenced by several scientific revelations that gradually tore religious mythology, as a metaphorical answer to the ends of human existence and the existence of god, from its pedestal and fuelled even more the scientific thirst for knowledge.[4] Thereby, natural sciences influenced philosophy, philosophy influenced economics, economics influenced biology and vice versa. The more insights gained, the more mankind thought to come closer to a complete understanding of the functioning of the world. Figure 5.1 is meant to summarize the parallels and cross-fertilization effects of various disciplines. Such a short inquiry can never be complete nor start at the ultimate origin. For the purpose here, suffice it to start as follows:

Rationalism vs. empiricism, a reconciliation and the persistence of the Newtonian world

Descartes (1596 – 1650) was the first philosopher who refrained from the clerical dominance and advocated to trust one's own rationality and thus introduced rationalism. His attempt was to develop a system of thoughts on mathematical grounds, giving a precise and complete account of all natural phenomena, reduced to their gist, with absolute mathematical certainty. The Physiocrats, as discussed in section 1.2, complied to the implications of a Cartesian[5] system as well as, a century later, classical economists such as Smith, Ricardo, Malthus, etc. tried in vain to construct a coherent and consistent economic theory in the realm of the Cartesian construct.

A full mathematical account of nature was developed by Newton; his mechanics became the "obstetrician" of the neoclassical paradigm. Newton gave the Cartesian world a mathematical formulation and it was only a matter of time until Newtonian mechanics became the heart of neoclassical methodology, although some necessary assumptions had to be accepted implicitly: every agent has to have full understanding of cause and effect; every agent necessarily has to own the innate capacity to access substantial reality all alone by cognition, so that aim-oriented behavior renders optimality.

In the 17th century, however, British philosophers rejected the idea that mankind could access reality solely by rational reasoning as suggested by

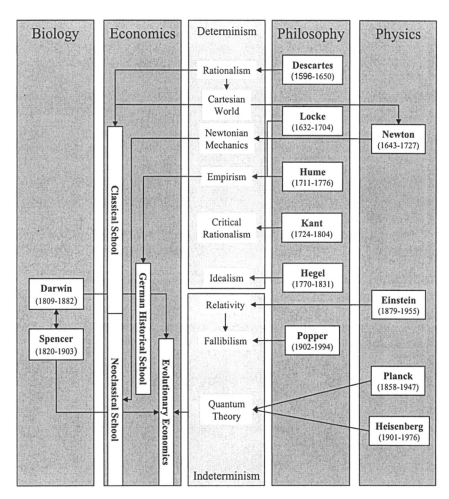

Figure 5.1: An overview of the philosophy of science.

mathematics. **John Locke** (1632 – 1704) objected to the proposition of god-given, logical principles and moral norms; instead, he saw human consciousness as a *tabula rasa* that generates ideas by experience which lead to further ideas by *reflection*.[6]

Besides the methodological question of epistemology in general, this view had also some implications for theorizing on human behavior in particular. Rational agents act best to their knowledge. For Locke, knowledge is a sensation which an individual experiences within himself. Consequently, the question arises whether there is an outside reality that corresponds to the individual's internal representation and whether that reality can actually be known by the individual. To his mind, the individual's subjective and internal representation is at least supported by the existence of substance and causality. From an epistemological point of view, this concept advocates empirical investigation. Concerning human behavior, as knowledge is subjective, the predictability of human behavior is restricted.

Empiricism, as this strand of philosophy is called, was taken to an extreme by **David Hume** (1711 – 1776) who disconnected factual reality from human cognition. He altered Locke's concept by denying the existence of substance and axiomatic causality.[7] It is habit that makes individuals believe that repetitively perceived connections represent reality and therefore suggest generally valid causalities. In other words, as long as we observe a certain connection between two "things", we think that it must be the objective truth. According to Hume, this conclusion cannot be drawn. Knowledge is based on experience and experience does not imply that a subjective view (i.e. knowledge) will be confirmed in the future and therefore has no ontological foundation.[8]

In economics, again with a bit of a time lag, it was the **German Historical School** which took a positivist position. It denied a priori knowledge and the knowledge of general axioms. Empiricism would be the key to access the real world,[9] hence, knowledge and (economic) behavior would be the result of experience, and thus doubt was cast on the neoclassical rationality postulate.

Immanuel Kant (1724 – 1804) formulated a synthesis of both views, empiricism and rationalism. On the one hand, he vehemently criticized empiricism that denies the possibility of axiomatic knowledge. On the other hand, he contrasted a dogmatic view of rationalism: in the 18th century, Kant showed that self-organization of living organisms cannot be explained by a Newtonian mechanical system. There are *analytical judgements* which are true a priori.[10] All other judgements are *synthetic* ones; they ask for empirical validation.[11] Kant's critical rationalism[12] was worked out by **Georg W. F. Hegel** (1770 – 1831), saying that the evolution of human mankind is determined by a dialectic process, thesis and antithesis, which leads to a synthesis, and therefore to a progress to a higher predetermined level called idealism.[13]

At the end of the 19th century, these two extreme philosophical views, rationalism versus radical, empirical scepticism, were also the subject matter of the so-called *Methodenstreit* in economics. The *älterer Methodenstreit* was a discussion about which method to prefer, induction versus deduction. The *jüngerer Methodenstreit* was about to what extent economics can give normative propositions at all.[14] One of those discussants was Menger, the founder of the Austrian school, who supported deduction. He inaugurated the marginal school and thus contributed to the neoclassical paradigm. But in the course of time, neoclassics and the Austrian tradition took a divergent path:[15] Both views are definitely Cartesian in a sense that they stipulate, from a epistemological perspective, the validity of known causes and effects; but they are different with respect to the following: the neoclassical school has remained Newtonian, whereas the Austrian school has taken into account the Kantian critique on Newtonian mechanics.[16]

Determinism versus Indeterminism   Despite the common base of neoclassical and Austrian-type economics, the neoclassical school has won the race. The reason seems to be straightforward, since neoclassical methodology itself is straightforward. It is reductionist and simple because it is deterministic. It is linear but not complex; unequivocal, normative though not open; all in all, it is idealistic and pragmatic, so that it had to become orthodoxy in economics. As figure 5.1 shows, determinism is prevailing as an implicit assumption in all sciences. This is not surprising, since determinism is a necessary condition, a prerequisite for guided research to come up with generally valid propositions. Up to that point in time, especially the findings in natural sciences seemed promising enough to come closer and closer to a comprehensive understanding of the world in its very nature. However, with Albert Einstein, who refrained from absolute propositions by introducing his relativity theory, the edifice of a deterministic world gradually crumbled. Einstein also inspired Karl Popper, who took up on the Humian idea that the objectivity of normative propositions does not have an ontological foundation. Popper sustained that the mental representation of reality is subjective and it will hardly ever be possible to verify such general propositions. All that any science can do is to deduce falsifiable hypotheses. Thereby, the refutation of those hypotheses is the principle task of scientists. Hypotheses which could not be falsified for a long time he calls *corroborated* but not necessarily true. Progress in science is achieved when long-term hypotheses could finally be rejected as Einstein's relativity theory rejected Newtonian physics, so that new hypotheses can be formed. Popper objects to rationalism as well as empiricism.[17] The influence of his fallibilism on economics is self-explanatory as

Popper's work is part of any introductory course in economics. He put the possibility to derive generally valid propositions into perspective so that the necessity to forebear indeterminism became more and more obvious.

Philosophy mirrors the linkage of all sciences. The findings in natural sciences, especially physics, motivated philosophy to find adequate answers. Once a philosophical framework had been constructed, social sciences fancied those ideas and adopted them for its own purpose. The success of neoclassical economics was stimulated by the findings in natural sciences at the end of the 19th century. When we indulge in the tempting fallacy, according to Hume, and let the habit of repetitively experienced sensations make us believe that this causality continues and the philosophical implications of modern natural sciences might again stimulate economic theorizing, then it seems straightforward to look at new findings and developments in modern philosophy in order to anticipate the future path of economics.

The most challenging observations of the 20th century were made in physics, observations that subsequently raised some major questions in philosophy. It is talked about as a new paradigm that turns classical physics upside down, a paradigm that makes the world indeterministic. Unfortunately, this new paradigm is an accumulation of endless questions rather than an offer of an alternative toolbox for heterodox (evolutionary) economics. Nevertheless, it might give us some useful hints for economic modelling. It is quantum theory that casts doubt on established epistemological and metaphysical concepts and clearly rejects determinism. It is not necessary to undergo the entire analysis of quantum physics for the purpose of this work, but it will make things easier to comprehend, therefore an intuitive explanation of the quantum theory is given in the appendix A. Although, the quantum theory has not yet provided a comprehensive explanation for its puzzling insights, it offers some implications that has to be taken into account in evolutionary economic theory.

Quantum theory   brings in *subjectivity*. It stresses the role of the investigator of a subject matter. The observer does not simply perceive a certain scenario but causes a *reciprocity* between the macroscopic environment (the observer and its methodological procedure) and the subject matter under investigation. Henceforth, the investigator partly plays the role of a *creator* so that reality becomes the intermingling result of *"objective" perception* and *subjective cognition*. Thus, natural and social sciences[18] are elevated onto a common denominator. The laws of nature, gained via experimental physics, all of a sudden become axiomatic assumptions – concessions social sciences had to struggle with ever since. Similarly, quantum physics addresses the *locality* of phenomena, which contextually react within a certain method of observation, and at the same time it allows the recognition of *non-local, macroscopic* phenomena transcendent to time and space. That is what the idea of the superposition (particle/wave) suggests.[19] Furthermore, the idea of superposition suggests, contrarily to Newtonian mechanics, that we do not have a complete set of particles and properties but that we do have a set of possible properties of which some will never come into existence, such as the simultaneous observation of the location and velocity of a particle;[20] the existence of different sets of possible properties is *complementary*, a once observed definite state of a property does not necessarily imply that it will show the same property again in future. The future is *indeterministic* and *unpredictable* but *open* for *creativity* and *novelty*. We are situated in a *probabilistic* world in which we observe *random behavior* on a micro level and apparently *quasi-deterministic behavior* on a macro level. In other words, the whole is not just the sum of its parts but it is more as we observe *symmetry breaking*. It is a *dynamic, unstable system* which is governed by the *non-linearity* of a *complex* world.

Quantum theory questions traditional methodology in physics as much as evolutionary economics questions orthodox economic methodology. In the following section, the parallels in economics are elaborated further. Hereby the term evolutionary economics is referred to. Eventually a synthesis in chapter 6 will merge implications of quantum theory with a sound evolutionary setting to model entrepreneurial behavior.

5.3 The Mystery/Misery of Evolutionary Economics

The closer we get to the intellectual frontier of contemporary heterodox economics, the more elusive the path of economics gets. We started out our journey through the history of economics with the phenomenon of entrepreneurship in economic theory. We realized that this issue is not only a question of the analysis of the entrepreneur in particular, but also the question of economic methodology in general. Furthermore, we saw the evolution of philosophy and its delayed impact on economics until we arrived in the 20th century. The more insights we gained along that path, the more questions emerged. If we really intend to answer those questions and if we do not want to run the risk of rephrasing old stories of economics over and over again, we need to change our way of thinking. This is easier said than done. Criticizing neoclassical theory turns out to be a simple task: we just discuss the framework of assumptions and subsequently question methodology. To come up with a constructive alternative approach, however, proves to be a complicated challenge. No wonder that heterodox approaches are manifold; the term evolutionary economics has become popular in use and comes closest to a generic term of heterodox economics, but it seems to be impossible to give an exact definition adequate to subsume the common imagination of all economists using this term.

Over and over again, the evolutionary metaphor is mentioned in economic literature. Alfred Marshall, a dyed-in-the-wool neoclassical economist himself, puts forward such an alternative approach, addressing the deficiencies of neoclassical mechanisms:

> *The Mecca of the economist lies in economic biology rather than in economic dynamics. But biological conceptions are more complex than those of mechanics; a volume on foundations must therefore give a relatively large place to mechanical analogies; and frequent use is made of the term "equilibrium," which suggests something of statical analogy. This fact, combined with the predominant attention paid in the present volume to the normal conditions of life in the modern age, has suggested the notion that its central idea is "statical," rather than "dynamical." But in fact it is concerned throughout with the forces that cause movement: and its key-note is that of dynamics, rather than statics.*[21]

Besides Marshall, many other economists came across the term 'evolutionary'.[22] Veblen (1898) discussed the evolutionary metaphor, whereas he linked this term to *institutionalism*.[23] The Austrian School is considered to be evolutionary, whereupon – most adjacently – the biological connotation served as an analogy.[24] Schumpeter emphasized the necessity to take into account evolutionary aspects in economic theorizing but contrarily rejected the biological concept.[25]

Each of these strands of thought would assert to be disjunct from each other but, at the same time, claim to be evolutionary. Hodgson (2000) undertakes a detailed survey about evolutionary theory with the resulting resignation that

> *(...) the word 'evolutionary' is extremely vague. It is now widely used, even by economists using neoclassical techniques. "Evolutionary game theory" is highly fashionable. Even Walras is described as an evolutionary economist (Jolink (1996)). (...) In precise terms it signifies little or nothing.*[26]

Conclusively, the definition of evolutionary economics is reduced to an undeterminable complement of orthodox neoclassical theory. So it is not surprising that there is no consistent way of doing evolutionary economics. Their common feature is the critique on neoclassical theory and the consequential intention to do things differently.

In chapter 2 we saw how the neoclassical edifice has been built, how the perfect rationality postulate became the foundation of the assumptional scaffolding on which its methodology spans. The path of criticism sketches forward. When we relax the rationality postulate, saying that actors neither have perfect information/foresight nor perfect capabilities we end up with bounded rationality.[27] Removing the foundation, we have to disassemble the scaffolding of the remaining assumptions and henceforth question the formal Newtonian methodology. Perfect rationality made it possible to assume optimal behavior denying true uncertainty.[28] Any contingencies the future might bring are parameterizable with probabilities in order to calculate expected values so that at least a breeze of indeterminism can be integrated into a de facto deterministic world. Determinism, however, requires completeness. All elements and connections within the economic system have to be known, but completeness simultaneously means a closed system which allows for a general equilibrium. Thus, Newtonian mechanics is legitimized in methodology to render the idea of predictability via normative theories. It is self-explanatory to call this concept static, leaving no space for creativity and novelty, no possibility for change, and therefore no right to exist for the entrepreneur.

With bounded rationality, however, the argumentation looks different. With bounded rationality, we end up with imperfect economic actors, actors without perfect information, foresight and capabilities. Thus we allow for true uncertainty but lose – at least to some extent – predictability of economic behavior, since we get in addition heterogeneous actors.[29] Instead of having perfect rational actors, who are no different from each other, they are not homogeneous. Since there is no definite state of imperfection, imperfect actors have to be heterogeneous in their specificities. Actors are not able to optimize any longer, they might not even be able to determine an optimal path ex post; they have to evaluate their actions themselves to eventually reach a state of *satisfaction*. Obviously, this makes the framework of assumptions rather *realistic* but also the economic system indeterminate and unpredictable. In such a system there is room for novelty. It is not an Homo economicus acting in a completely transparent and closed system but it is a passionate, lively human being that has the option to discover novelties in "*(...) an economic universe that is fundamentally open-ended in its possibilities(...).*"[30] It is open to creativity. The latter also shows up in the different perspectives of heterodox (evolutionary) approaches. Again, the common denominator of heterodox economics is the critique on neoclassical assumptions. Unfortunately, criticism alone does not automatically provide for an adequate methodology. Institutionalism,

Neo-Schumpeterian economics, the biological metaphor, etc. paraphrase the trial-and-error process in economic theory to eventually find an alternative heterodox approach, an approach different to the neoclassical one but as specific as the neoclassical paradigm. Followers of Veblen[31] tie their evolutionary framework to an institutional context. Schumpeter's conception is associated with innovation.[32] When using a biological metaphor, it referred to the Darwinian/Lamarckian evolutionary biology,[33] whereby it is not yet clear to which extent such an analogy is useful to explain human economic behavior.[34] In other words, it still has to be managed to develop a standardizing body in methodology to flesh out the term 'evolutionary' with a consolidated economic (evolutionary) paradigm.[35]

As far as one can say, despite the detours and turnarounds in evolutionary economics, the common ground of evolutionary thinking looks as follows: Evolutionary economics[36] refers to a theory

- that is based on *heterogeneity*,[37] which is

- transformed via a *dynamic process*, i.e. a *coordinating, selective process* into a

- pattern of *economic change*;[38]

- takes into account *historic time* and *irreversibility* of *economic development*, and

- allows for *novelty*.[39]

Up to this point, the paradigm of evolutionary economics and its difficulties in practice have been addressed. Next, a synthesis between the implications of quantum mechanics and some basic evolutionary principles is undertaken, to develop the methodological setting for the entrepreneurship model which will finally be constructed in this work.

Notes

[1] See chapter 1 for a detailed discussion of neoclassical assumptions and their contradiction to an entrepreneur in such theory.

[2] Evolutionary economics has become a popular term in economic theory. But as we will see later on, this term has probably become the most unlucky choice to subsume the need for heterodoxy in economics. It has a lot of different connotations. In this work it is used as a collective term for heterodox economics.

[3] There are many parallels between economics and philosophy and it is impossible to disentangle the mutual fertilization of these two disciplines. To mention one obvious parallel,

we can detect this linkage in *utilitarism*. It was Jeremy Bentham (1789) who initiated utilitarism in economics. Individuals' actions are driven by *pain* and *pleasure*, a concept Hume had already worked on. John Stuart Mill (1962) refined and expanded Bentham's ideas. Till the beginning of the marginal school, and along with Jevons, Walras and Menger, all nuances of utility and its importance for economic behavior had been discussed in detail. See section 5.2.

[4] As an example, Kopernikus dislocated mankind out of the middle of the universe. Darwin sensed the human species as a random product of evolution. Freud imputed human self-determination with a sexual motivation. And many more scientific disclosures spurred philosophy, spurred the human need to discover the truth about the existence of human mankind. The search for a better understanding of the world, the search for general propositions, for principles, for axioms that could be based on absolute certainty.

[5] See Mainzer (1996b, p. 248).

[6] Compare Locke (1690).

[7] He distinguished *impressions* from *ideas*. The former were the direct sensual perceptions, the latter the individuals cognitive representation. Conclusively, every mental connection of ideas, an individual makes, is a subjective, mental construct. Compare Hume (1748).

[8] This extreme negation of an objective reality and the concept of subjectivism is also referred to as *radical constructivism*.

[9] Realism suggests that reality exists independent of human consciousness and perception.

[10] For example, to deny the proposition "It is raining or it is not" would be a contradiction in itself. Hence, this statement is analytically true.

[11] The fact that water boils at 100 degrees centigrade cannot be proved analytically, but by empirical investigation.

[12] Compare Kant (1884).

[13] Compare Hegel (1996).

[14] This would come close to the sceptical empiricism of Hume. See Kolb (1991, p. 15)

[15] See chapter 3 to make this comparison.

[16] In figure 5.1 the Austrian school is subsumed under the term "evolutionary economics".

[17] Compare Popper (1959).

[18] Compare Penrose (1990) and Zohar (1990)

[19] See appendix A.

[20] In physics this is referred to as Heisenberg's uncertainty principle.

[21] Marshall (1948, p. 19).

[22] See for example Dosi (1991, p. 5), Hodgson (1998, p. 160) or Foster and Stanley (2001).

[23] Also the work that relates to institutionalism is associated with evolutionary economics. See for example Hodgson (1995b, p. xv).

[24] Menger and Hayek introduced many biological terms into their work. See Hodgson (1998, p. 160). And still, the biological metaphor very often serves modern evolutionary thinking. See also Nelson and Winter (1982) and Foster and Stanley (2001).

[25] Compare Hanusch (1988), Shionoya (1998, p. 437) among others.

[26] Hodgson (2000).

[27] Compare Simon and Egidi (1992).

[28] Compare Knight (1921).

[29] This illustrates most obviously the closeness to the biological metaphor entering the economic discussion, concerning heterogeneity, variety, population thinking, etc. See for example Hirschleifer (1982).

[30] Foss (1994, p. 22).

[31] See Dopfer (1986a), Dopfer (1986b) and De Bresson (1987).

[32] See Hanusch (1988).

[33] Compare figure 5.1 on page 51.

[34] See Caplan (1978), Corning (1996), Wilson (1998), Hodgson (1995a), Hodgson (2002) for further exemplary attempts and thoughts on *biology and economics*.

[35] Dopfer (2001) gives a collection of seminal contributions towards this attempt.

[36] For a succinct setting of an evolutionary theory, see for example Nelson (1995).

[37] Metcalfe (1994a), Metcalfe (1994b), Metcalfe, Fonseca and Ramlogan (2000), Saviotti (1996), Cantner (1996) and Cantner and Hanusch (2001) stress the role of heterogeneity as the ultimate source of any evolutionary development.

[38] See Metcalfe et al. (2000, p. 2).

[39] Witt (1987, p. 9) may serve as one out of many possible references.

6 Synthesis of Evolutionary Ideas

6.1 Consolidating Thoughts

What we learn from the history of economics, natural sciences and philosophy Summarizing the preceding elaborations, we detected parallels between philosophy, natural as well as social sciences (focusing on economics). All try to generate general propositions, or even better, stable and generally valid axioms about the subject matter under investigation. At the end of the 19th century, natural sciences seemed to be on the verge of a comprehensive description of a deterministic world.[1] Social sciences and in particular economics have always been struggling to model analogously a deterministic world; in economics the outcome has become known as neoclassical economics. The scope of experimental economics is fairly narrow; at the most, very specific micro-level, i.e. rather psychological/sociological phenomena are "testable" in laboratory-like conditions. But they hardly ever deliver generally valid axioms as classical physics is suggesting. Social and in particular economic phenomena seem to be no constant ones. The 20th century, however, turned classical physics upside down and henceforth physics was burdened by Hume's (philosophical) reservation, which social science has always been struggling with: ideas, generated by reflections on perceived impressions, are a mental construct of the observer and therefore partially an artefact. (Classical) physics, on the other hand, seemed to be able to make irrevocable statements, i.e. axioms that picture a stable, linear and non-dynamic world. Quantum theory put experimental phenomena into the perspective of the observer, so that experimental results apparently become biased.[2] Modern physics challenges modern philosophy and at the same time parallels modern (evolutionary) economics, which was outlined in chapter 5. The need for heterodoxy is obvious, but to be different and specific all at once turns out to be difficult.

The question now is, how to bring in line intuition, theory, empirical observations on a common methodological ground, thereby taking into account the work done so far, and not simply retelling but hopefully contributing new aspects to the subject chosen for investigation. Against the background of the history of economic thought and the disillusioning revelations in natural sciences subsuming the puzzling questions of epistemology and ontology in philosophy, the attempt to come closer to a Cartesian (Newtonian) formulation of the world is becoming more and more elusive; a world of precise interdependencies and causalities to derive behavioral instructions for an ultimate convergence of intentional and actual outcomes of human behavior, can this be an accomplishable goal to pursue, or will it turn out to be a persistent fallacy of science?

Do we have to assume a deterministic world, a world of rationalism so that we end up with a neoclassical paradigm and thus buy predictability (normative theory) at the cost of a doubtfully idealized world? Or do we have to do economics totally without a tiny bit of determinism so that we have to accept a nihilistic chaos of indeterminacy, which at best allows for a purely descriptive economic theory? Presumably, the answer must lie somewhere in between, but where? We definitely have to give up the general claim for a normative theory until we find, if ever, the "real" underlying causalities that allow for such theory. Some normative theories function quite well in economic reality, so that there might be no need to change anything, whereas others, e.g. entrepreneurship theories, do not work at all in a normative framework. The search for the entrepreneur in economics seems to raise the same puzzling questions as quantum theory does in physics. We know that there is entrepreneurial behavior which brings along innovation and economic change. But when we look at the specificities of an idealized entrepreneur, we are not able to figure out his detailed profile. There is an indeterminacy phenomenon similar to the particle–wave duality in quantum theory: we observe the light wave but cannot observe the photon's locality and impulse at the same time. Newtonian mechanics proves to be inadequate to cope such phenomenon and therefore asks for an alternative treatment.

In the following, the attempt is made to give a convergence of the eclectic ideas collected above in order to propose a possible approach.

Although we have to give up traditional (neoclassical) methodology to model entrepreneurship, we can take the underlying **intuition** which is independent of methodology. The French and the Austrian school offer this option. A suitable methodology still has to be developed. Aspects and analogies to philosophy and natural sciences will inspire a first attempt towards an alternative approach which will be evolutionary. To prevent a possibly unfortunate interpretation of this "evolutionary concept", it has to be emphasized that in this work, although it refers to various kinds of analogies from all strands of science, the intention is to establish a concept, independent, and primarily, with a focus on the economic perspective and not with a bias to some analogy such as biology or - as some readers might think - quantum theory. Those analogies are helpful to get an idea but also run the risk to get overanalyzed, neglecting the focus on economic behavior performed by aim-oriented human beings.

The first important question to answer is the question about the ontological foundation of an evolutionary approach. The methodological reflections of Hermann-Pillath (2001) on neoclassical growth theory illustrates the necessary ontological foundation of such a concept: Any theory has to make a reference to reality.[3] Considering growth theory Hermann-Pillath (2001) states: *"The production function is the only statement with reference to reality."*[4] Hence, any empirical evidence reduces to testing the validity of the production function itself. As we saw above, however, the production function is a mental construct, abstracted from the ontological assumption of perfect rational agents. Therefore, according to Hermann-Pillath (2001), this neglects the

> *[h]uman mind [, which] must be an integral part of any on-*
> *tology of economics. [Furthermore,](...) ontology entertains*
> *a reflective relationship with ontology. There is no way to*
> *pull the scientific observer out of the world. We will therefore*
> *speak of a 'bimodal reality' of mind and world and hence a*
> *'bimodal ontology' (compare Dopfer, 1990b). Mind is an el-*
> *ement of the world but at the same time a mirror of the world*
> *guiding human action within the world, including the scien-*
> *tific observer's action.*[5]

A bimodal reality allows for a discrepancy between the agents' mental representation of the world and reality, which necessarily incorporates bounded rationality, learning and the role of (fallible) knowledge into economic theory.[6] Consequently, evolutionary economics has to link the human mind with reality and, with it, integrate the fallibility of human thinking since the human mind takes a dual position is such world; an epistemological and an ontological one.[7] Subsequently, the idea suggests itself that the intention in traditional economics to separate its theoretical foundation from other behavioral sciences, such as psychology, can no longer be maintained. The **openness** of the economic system is another consequence of a bimodal ontology, i.e. the fact of the human mind's fallibility. The mental representation of reality may differ tremendously among individuals. There is a multitude of different possible states in human mind, states that one may call **knowledge**.[8] Apart from ostensibly **heterogeneous** preferences of individuals, human behavior will differ solely because of these different states of knowledge; we might even observe **singularities** in behavior, and, presupposing adaptive actors, also a change over time. Obviously, the basic evolutionary setting cannot be a closed Cartesian system, even less a Newtonian one. On the contrary, the world is not simply the sum of singularities, either. Theories about singular phenomena would be useless since they are impossible according to Aristotle.[9] In analogy to quantum theory, the singularity problem can be tolerated: the **system duality**, which is inherent to the **superposition** particle/wave, suggests a **local** contextual quasi-random behavior, which can be interpreted as a singularity, (Heisenberg's uncertainty principle) but on the other hand, it proposes also the existence of **non-local** phenomena,[10] which suggests the existence of general phenomena despite stochastically independent, local events. In economic terms: although micro behavior might be perceived as random, but independent, similar events (general phenomena) are observed on a macro level. This advocates the connection between the micro and the meso/macro level. Besides, Heisenberg's uncertainty principle also stipulates **symmetry breaking**, since the transition from particle to wave apparently is not observable. Analogously in economics, ascending the aggregation level from the micro- to the macro-level we have to take into account symmetry breaking within economic behavior. An isolated human being acts in accordance with his psychology. Within the context of a social group, however, his behavior might change depending on the sociology of the group. The environment of a firm might change his behavior even more when more and more compelling, formal institutions make him behave in a certain manner. Between each step we observe a symmetry breaking, which makes the aggregation from the micro to the macro level difficult.

Figure 6.1 illustrates the systematics. Heisenberg's uncertainty principle[11] serves as an analogue to give economic thinking a different twist. Above, the heterogeneity of the human mind and consequently, the heterogeneity of human beings was stated. Some economic behaviors might be explicable to economists but some, and the decision to engage in entrepreneurial activity belongs to those, seem to be quasi-random phenomena.

Quasi-randomness means that there are determinants that support a certain economic behavior, but we simply cannot figure out for example what exactly makes an entrepreneur. Therefore, looking at a specific individual a possible entrepreneurial decision is quasi random. Each individual has a certain propensity to become an entrepreneur,[12] but it is not a deterministic characteristic of the individual. It is a singular (local) phenomenon once an individual undertakes entrepreneurial actions. Apart from the individual's psychology (personality), the social context is a further determinant of economic actions.

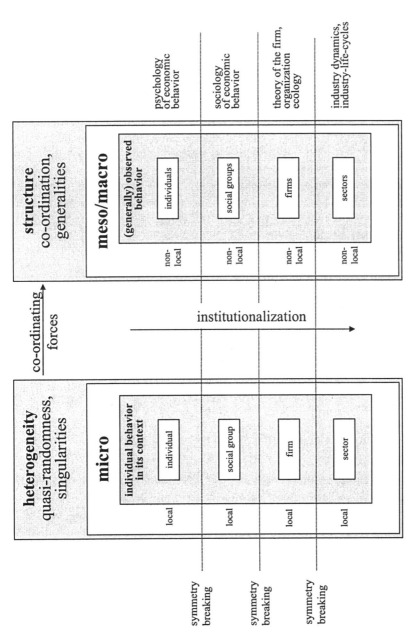

Figure 6.1: Heisenberg's uncertainty principle adapted to economics.

The decisions an individual makes in isolation will differ from decisions made in a certain social context. This is what we call symmetry breaking. It is the sociology of a group that prohibits the conclusion from the individual's behavior in isolation to the behavior of the entire social group.[13] It is not simply the sum of the parts that represents the whole. When we expand this thread, we detect another symmetry breaking towards the behavior within a firm, etc. Since the necessity of institutionalized behavior gets more and more compelling, actors' behavior will differ along this train of thoughts and the aggregation of individual behavior becomes more and more difficult when we do not want to neglect the fact of heterogeneous, local behavior and symmetry breaking. The latter makes one assume that we have to deal with a rather chaotic system. Empirical work, however, shows us that there must be some **coordinating forces** within the system. Though we observe local singularities, i.e. singular behavior of individuals, we observe a coordinated structure on a higher level, on a meso/macro level.[14] Somehow the heterogeneity transforms into a structure, into a non-local, general phenomenon.

Human behavior is neither deterministic nor completely chaotic. Despite the complexity of such a system, comprising heterogeneity and symmetry breaking, we have to assume causal behavior of rational agents albeit bounded rational ones. Some causalities might be obvious to the actor as well as the scientific observer, whereas others seem to be "non-causal" phenomena, which either denote quasi-random behavior under true uncertainty, or simply the inaccessibility of individuals' internal motives to the observer. But there is **guidance** within the system. The fact of life is, and that is what economics is all about, that humankind has to deal with scarce resources and is burdened by uncertainty. The individual acts according to his knowledge, according to his belief of cause and effect, which need not reflect reality. Human behavior is subject to error, but it is **aim-oriented** though not deterministic as supposed by a perfect rationality postulate.

Menger, among others, gave an implicit concept of an aim-oriented economic action. His theory on value[15] gives us the guide posts of economic behavior. The human beings' needs and their knowledge how to satisfy these needs, given a certain amount of owned resources, are the driving forces of human action. Knowledge, therefore, plays an important role; it contains a multitude of perspectives. As mentioned above, the bimodal reality introduces fallibility of behavior and the importance of the human's capacity to learn, but knowledge is not only about technology, it is the individual's mental representation of reality and its functioning. Learning signifies the adaptation process in which the individual's mental representation of the world gets adjusted to reality. The individual learns about technology, but also about the economic behavior of others. Learning is a dynamic process, since economic behavior is an interactive and interdependent process among individuals. It is necessary for individuals to evaluate the potential behavior of others and thus the economic situation. For example, a potential entrepreneur has to evaluate whether there is a market for the goods or services he wants to sell, whether he will stand future competition, whether there might be proper funding for his venture, etc.[16] So it is even more important to know the beliefs of others about reality than reality itself and to anticipate e.g. consumers' behavior. On account of the duality of human mind being an ontological element of the economic reality as well as the epistemological instrument to access reality, the actor takes an ambiguous role. First, he observes past and present economic behavior and interprets it accordingly to adjust his actions. Second, he takes the chance to influence actual economic behavior with actions (e.g. actions of market-making). He influences the individuals' mental representation and thus influences their actions. Conclusively, he influences reality and, similar to quantum theory, the actor as an observer becomes a *creator* of (economic) reality. Furthermore, this reciprocity makes the consideration of *feedback processes* essential to any such theory.

To sum up, because of local phenomena, heterogeneity and symmetry breaking, we have to deal with a probabilistic system. With the bimodal ontology of the human mind, the subsequent reciprocity asks for feedback processes within such theory; feedback processes between the observer and the observed, between local and non-local phenomena, between the meso/macro and the micro level, between the whole and the single elements of the system. As we cannot cover all causalities within a single theory – then, it would not be anymore a simple model but complex reality – we have to focus on a certain part such as the micro-level analyzing e.g. entrepreneurial behavior. Moreover, because of the reciprocity and feedback effects we cannot do partial analysis but we have to look at the whole system in order not to neglect important interdependencies necessary to explain the subject matter (holistic perspective). Obviously we have to make assumptions but no strict assumptions on the individuals' level to smother any chance for innovative behavior.

In the following section, a possible instrument will be discussed, which allows to model a theory on grounds of the evolutionary setting derived above: an open system that allows for novelty and creativity; a complex non-deterministic system that gives a sound standing for an endogenous dynamic of economic change.

6.2 Graph Theory: A First Step Towards an Evolutionary Methodology

Owing to the criticism on the neoclassical methodology, an alternative approach has to be found in order to structure the procedure of evolutionary modelling. Indeed, there are various tools that are used in evolutionary literature. At the present stage of evolutionary economics, as far as the author is apt to judge, a least compelling tool has to be applied to also keep the evolution of methodology open. A procedure has been selected which has already been put forward by others. More will be given later.

Jason Potts (2000) in his seminal work on *The New Evolutionary Microeconomics* elaborated a useful apparatus to substantiate the evolutionary concept with a formal application, an application which critically differs from standard neoclassical methodology and sounds promising for evolutionary model makers. Potts also discusses traditional methodology and, among other things, focuses in his discourse on field theory as it is applied in neoclassical analysis: field theory usually defines the logical space of traditional economic theory. The $\mathbb{R}^n$ spans the *canvas* the economist (artist) paints his theory on, and hardly ever questions the adequacy of such subsurface. *Neowalrasian economic theory* is defined over such real field. The $\mathbb{R}^n$, however, is a space in which every element has a unique position and a relation to all other elements within the space, all points are connected with each other. Hence, the $\mathbb{R}^n$ represents a Cartesian world. It is a complete, closed and deterministic subordinate to Newtonian mechanics. So, the theoretic painting cannot live up to its promise:

> *There is excess demand, but there are no trades; there is a price system, but there are no markets; there are agents and actions, but no events are observable; there are shares in production, but production does not occur. I have been told that these and other 'anomalies' in neowalrasian theory are 'just a matter of semantics'. I do not disagree; but I am bound to reflect that science is concerned with little else.*[17]

Excessive demand, trades, markets, etc. are real world phenomena, which are mere metaphors of disequilibrium in equilibrium analysis. In the neowalrasian world, the idea is to start right after all adjustment processes towards equilibrium have already been completed, i.e. to start with equilibrium. Then, the result is a Cartesian system which allows to use field theory. Every element and every interaction between elements is expressed in functional forms that map the $\mathbb{R}^n$ to the $\mathbb{R}^n$ space. Hence, the $\mathbb{R}^n$ is a complete set of interactions; as a consequence, economic actors have to have complete information and foresight that is perfect rationality.

But then, actual "(...) choice disappears; nothing is left but stimulus and response."[18] The nature of a field is to be an integral concept but the geometry of the economic space is a non-integral one. Not all connections between the elements of an economic system do actually exist. That is what Shackle (1972), O'Driscoll and Rizzo (1986) refer to when they talk about *time*: the existence of *uncertainty* and *ignorance*; aspects, which indeed cast doubt on the existence of an equilibrium, whose existence,[19] in return, is irrelevant to the context of field theory.[20]

When we want to describe real-world phenomena, when we want to investigate economic processes, we need to have a *language*. The neoclassical language is field theory as mentioned above. But any language is based on paradigmatic rules which is called grammar. It is impossible to formulate meaningful sentences which do not comply with those rules. The grammar of the neoclassical language is tied to the equilibrium paradigm and therefore, theorizing is confined to equilibrium phenomena, if such a thing ever exists. To go beyond the frontiers of equilibrium analysis, we have to find a proper language which is less constraining but open for phenomena we strive to investigate: uncertainty, economic change, innovation, entrepreneurship, etc. Graph theory looks promising to fulfill this claim.[21]

The basics of graph theory will be outlined briefly below. By doing this, the suitability of graph theory – as the evolutionary language – will come to the reader's mind self-explanatorily.

A graph G consists of a non-empty set of elements (vertices) V and a set of connections (edges) E,[22] which not only constitute a graph but also represent the two ontological foundations of an evolutionary model. These two ontological propositions that Potts (2000) puts forward are:

- *Evolutionary-HC1: There exists a set of elements.*

- *Evolutionary-HC2: There exists a set of connections.*[23]

Compared to the neoclassic theory, the number of necessary assumptions is reduced to these two propositions.[24] Instead of graph, we say *system* to come closer to an economic terminology, i.e. the economic system, $S = (V, E)$. The set of elements V looks as follows:

$$V = (v_1, \ldots, v_i, \ldots, v_n) \tag{6.1}$$

If two elements are connected, they are *adjacent*. The set of connections, E, that connects elements, i and j, denotes:

$$E = (e_{ij}, \ldots) \tag{6.2}$$

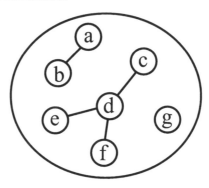

Figure 6.2: An economic system.
$$V = (a,b,c,d,e,f,g)$$
$$E = (ab,cd,de,df)$$

The number of an element's connections, k, determines its *degree*. In a *k-regular* system, each of the n elements has the same number of connections. The total number of connections determines the *size M* of the system, whereby:

$$M = \frac{nk}{2} \qquad (6.3)$$

A possible (economic) system is shown in figure 6.2.

The adjacency matrix $S(A)$ represents the connective structure of the system. It is a 7x7 triangular matrix with rows and columns which contain the elements V. A connection e_{ij} between two elements, i and j, which makes them *neighbors*, is symbolized by a 1 in the adjacency matrix $S(A)$, whereby an element is not connected to itself:

$$S(A) = \begin{bmatrix} 0 & 1 & 0 & 0 & 0 & 0 & 0 \\ 1 & 0 & 0 & 0 & 0 & 0 & 0 \\ 0 & 0 & 0 & 1 & 0 & 0 & 0 \\ 0 & 0 & 1 & 0 & 1 & 1 & 0 \\ 0 & 0 & 0 & 1 & 0 & 0 & 0 \\ 0 & 0 & 0 & 1 & 0 & 0 & 0 \\ 0 & 0 & 0 & 0 & 0 & 0 & 0 \end{bmatrix} \qquad (6.4)$$

The boundaries of all possible constellations of *state-space* are given by the two limiting cases – the *null system* and the *complete system*. The null system denotes a state-space when no element is connected to any other element. Interpreting connections as economic interaction, then, in a null system there are no interactions (figure 6.3).

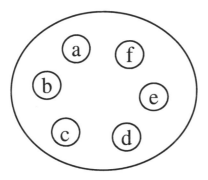

Figure 6.3: The null system.

The number of all possible states of a system depends on the number of elements. Kauffman (1993) states s distinct n-systems.

$$s = 2^n \tag{6.5}$$

A complete system denotes a state-space in which all elements are connected with each other. The adjacency matrix $S(A)$ then consists of only 1s except for the diagonal which is only made of 0s by definition. A complete system, as it is shown in figure 6.4, has the topology of a field.

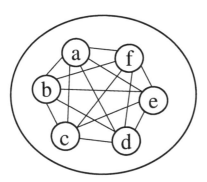

Figure 6.4: The complete system.

A system is incomplete as soon as $k < n$, and this is the general case in evolutionary economics, adversely to a complete system which is prescribed by field theory. Thus, an incomplete system is an adequate description of a non-integral space, an open system.

System-Element Duality and Hyperstructure   Graph theory not only supplies an easy way to describe economic interaction but also enables us to cope with the nature of emergence and hierarchy. Elements and connections embody a system, whereas the system in return may serve as an element for a higher-level system, and vice versa each element may itself be a system. This system–element duality allows to investigate the functioning of a system and how emerging higher-level systems build certain structures (hierarchies). Potts (2000) suggests to call this conception *hyperstructure*,[25] which merges the concept of emergence and hierarchy into a single construct.[26] Figure 6.1 in the previous section may serve as an example. The individual is an element of the system social group. A social group can be considered to be an element of the system "firm", whereby the firm is an element of the market system which is a three-level hyperstructure. In figure 6.5, the hyperstructured firm as an element of the market system is given.

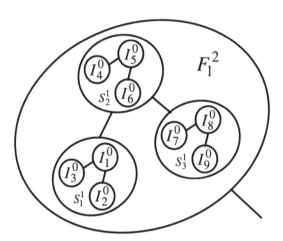

Figure 6.5: The hyperstructured firm.
Note: A system is a system of systems. E.g.: the firm F_1 is element 1 of a market system. The firm itself is a system of 3 social groups S_l^1, with $l = 1,2,3$. Each social group l is a system of individuals I_i^0, with $i = 1,2,...,7$. The superscript labels the emerging system level. Hence, we have a three-level hyperstructured system.

Complexity The idea of elements and connections, giving shape to the manifold states of a system, also allows to incorporate the notion of complexity. It is frequently used as an opposite to simplicity. Starting with von Neumann – one of the first who dealt with complexity – complexity is considered as a stereotypical characteristic of natural systems: to his mind, complexity is a measurable magnitude which occurs once a threshold has been exceeded and thus, a complex system differs from some kind of system which he assumed to be a simple one.[27] This understanding of complexity, however, does not explicitly ask for a different mathematical treatment than field theory. It is a more sophisticated conception of complexity that goes together with a graph theoretical approach. Unfortunately, there is no clear-cut definition of complexity. Rosen (1987) refers to physics (such as quantum theory) and faces simple, mechanistic systems with complex ones that allow for novelty, i.e. emergence. Prigogine (1987) also quotes physics as the first science that deals with complexity referring to thermodynamics which brings in entropy as a measure of information and disorder in a dynamic context. Not every initial state would lead to equilibrium. There are optional developments associated with self-organization processes which show possible bifurcation mechanisms and eventually lead to complexity and irreversible trajectories. Forrester (1987) focuses on nonlinearities of complex systems, whereas Boulding (1987) discusses the role of knowledge in this context.[28]

Irrespective of a unique definition, each of these concepts adopts a graph-theoretic approach. The matter of emerging phenomena has been discussed above. The null system and the complete system mark two extremes in state-space. In a null system there are no connections. Therefore, there are no interactions, no interdependencies; it is a state of perfect order. In a complete system, each element is connected to all other existing elements; it is a state of chaos in which any perturbation leads to chaotic behavior. In other words, the connective structure of a system determines its complexity. The degree of complexity is increasing with the number of connections within a system. It ranges from a state of perfect order, the null system, to a state of chaos, which is the complete system. Without any connections in a system, a change of an element in V does not affect any other element. With a complete set of connections (interactions/interdepenecies), any change of some element propagates to all other elements. This means extreme instability.

Considering human beings as social creatures, interacting with each other, the economic system is not a null system but a system with a connective structure. Adding heterogeneity of actors to social interaction, the connective structure of an economic system changes over time: new connections will be formed, old connections may be destroyed. Interactions shape the evolution of knowledge, preferences, institutions and technology.

In a general way, the basic setting of the evolutionary approach intended to be the meta-structure of the entrepreneurship model is given in the next part of this work. Proceeding with a concrete model, the notion of the constructed evolutionary scaffolding will become clearer.

Notes

[1] The (Newtonian) results seemed to be straightforward. Although many insights suggested the opposite, the imprint of a stable, deterministic, idealistic view of the world is persistent in the human mind. Take Einstein's relativity theory for example. He gave up the idea of an absolute measure of time and space. He claimed that natural laws would be stable from any point of view of the observer, independent of the speed of movement within space. It is the difference in the relative velocities of two observers that contradicts the axioms of classical physics such as an objective measure of time and space. Thus, he gave up a static concept of time and space. His general relativity theory reconciled the Newtonian law of gravitation and his special relativity theory for the sake of a static view of the world. Einstein maintained a deterministic position, though he would have been able to detect an overall dynamics. For more details see Hawking (1988).

[2] Concerning physics, it would be an interesting task to observe analogously to economics whether a *Methodenstreit* is unleashed and a period of "back-and-forth" physics is going on. But this is not the aim of this work.

[3] Compare Mäki (1998, p. 409) and Mäki (1989, p. 179).

[4] Hermann-Pillath (2001, p. 96).

[5] See Hermann-Pillath (2001, p. 98). Note: With this ontological claim of an evolutionary approach by Hermann-Pillath, we can detect two parallels: the interdependence between the human mind and reality discussed in philosophy (John Locke and David Hume) and the reciprocity between the observer and the subject matter observed in quantum theory.

[6] The Austrian School counts as a precursor of that tradition in economics, since the approach of Menger, Hayek, Mises, etc. pivots around knowledge within the market process.

[7] Compare Campbell (1987). The analogy to quantum theory is the notion about the reciprocity between the observer (apparatus) and the subject observed.

[8] Compare Hermann-Pillath (2001).

[9] Compare Hermann-Pillath (2001, p. 109).

[10] This discussion has become known as the quantum dice dispute in physics (Einstein, Planck, Schrödinger, Bohr, etc.). See details in Heisenberg (2000).

[11] To recall Heisenberg's uncertainty principle about the particle/wave issue: "The more precisely the position is determined, the less precisely the momentum is known." Be aware that any kind of comparison is a stretch.

[12] That is: It has the *superposition* entrepreneur/non-entrepreneur.

[13] Durlauf (1997), Brock and Durlauf (1999) give examples.

[14] Using another analogy for illustration: the second law of thermodynamics uses the same perspective.

[15] See chapter 3.

[16] See Porter (1980).

[17]Clower (1995, p. 314).

[18]Loasby (1976, p. 5).

[19]Compare Arrow and Debreu (1954).

[20]Compare Potts (2000, p. 23).

[21]Besides Potts (2000), Green (1996), Kauffman (1993), Kirman (1983) and Kirman (1987) have also recommended graph theory in their works.

[22]See Neumann and Morlock (1993) as an introduction.

[23]HC1 and HC2 mean hard-core proposition 1 and 2, respectively. Potts (2000, p. 56).

[24]Potts (2000, p. 57) confronts his evolutionary hard-core propositions with the ones in neoclassical theory, which are: HC1-There exist economic agents, HC2-Agents have preferences over outcomes, HC3-Agents independently optimize subject to constraints, HC4-Choices are made in interrelated markets, HC5-Agents have full relevant knowledge, HC6-Observable economic outcomes are coordinated, so they must be discussed with reference to equilibrium states. Propositions HC2-HC6 are necessary propositions to legitimize the application of field theory.

[25]The idea of hyperstructured systems was also discussed by Bertalanffy (1962) and Koestler (1969).

[26]Potts (2000, p. 68) refers to Baas (1994) and Baas (1997).

[27]Compare Rosen (1987).

[28]Potts (2000) enumerates many more references concerning complexity.

Part III

Modelling Entrepreneurship from an Evolutionary Perspective

7 Point of Departure

In this part an entrepreneurship model is developed taking into account the reflections from the previous chapters. The model is meant to be a general approach to entrepreneurship, delivering constructive propositions for a basic evolutionary setting. Furthermore, it provides the basis for a lot of possible expansions for future research.

To make things easier, the author's intuition about entrepreneurial behavior, observed in the Knowledge-based Economy, is given. After that, a short overview about subsequent chapters helps to put together the bits and pieces with respect to methodology, specific theories and the instruments used for modelling.

7.1 The Intuition on Entrepreneurial Behavior in the Knowledge-based Economy

As usual, any modelling effort starts with a basic intuition, with a basic idea about a subject matter. The initial spark of this project originates in the arrival of new information and communication technologies in the 1990's. The conglomerate of technologies which constitute the internet suggested an unprecedented innovation potential, obviously offering business opportunities for almost everyone. At an early stage, first firm foundations seemed promising and subsequently, spurred a wave of foundations. A fact that accounted for unexpected growth rates in GDP,[1] reducing unemployment to a considerable degree along a non-increasing inflation rate. An astonishing but desirable development which even tempted economists to label it the *New Economy*. It was the beginning of the Knowledge-based Economy that was heralded and would change economic processes.

From a scientific perspective, however, it is rather difficult to grasp what the Knowledge-based Economy is actually characterized by. Audretsch and Thurik (2000) categorize the specificities of the Knowledge-based Economy and enumerate various "trade-offs" such as *localization* versus *globalization, change* versus *continuity* or *turbulence* versus *stability*, etc. According to them knowledge-based economies are more globalized, more turbulent and are subject to a higher rate of economic change. Therefore, the Knowledge-based economy is also a highly entrepreneurial economy.

The specificities of the Knowledge-based Economy will not be discussed in detail here. It will do to state the basic characterization of the Knowledge-based Economy as an example for entrepreneurial behavior in an economy. The term "knowledge-based" stresses the fact that knowledge has become a more important input and output factor (yet not necessarily a generically new input and output factor), facilitated by modern information and communication technologies (ICTs). New ICTs have enhanced the transmissibility and exchange of information/knowledge in any economic sector. These technologies constitute a *general purpose technology* (GPT), a key technology that provides opportunities for numerous, successive innovations, i.e. entrepreneurial behavior and the birth of new firms. The internet, as the prime example of all ICTs, is the result of such a combination of various key technologies. The idea of a world-wide interconnectedness, which delivers the opportunity of a world-wide availability of knowledge and accessibility of customers, sowed the seeds for further incremental innovations, the creation of new knowledge. Thus, the hatchery of the "New Economy" was shaped and the "E-hype" followed in its wake.

The internet, as the result of several highly knowledge-intensive technologies, became an easy-to-use device, accessible with common, "John-Doe" knowledge. The internet has become the designated symbol for the surge of future process innovations waiting to come, since the transaction-cost-saving argument of the internet as a new distribution and communication channel was intuitively evident. Consequently, the E-market potential seemed almost infinite; the efficiency-improving qualities of the internet seemed obvious to everyone. Also, there was a quasi non-existing competition due to a very low number of incumbent firms in the E-market and negligible barriers to enter, so that the new GPT offered a high potential for innovation.

The easier the basics of such technology are understood by actors, the more potential entrepreneurs will emerge. At an early stage of the GPT, when entrants do not have to compete and catch up with long-term incumbent firms, which usually have achieved a competitive advantage by accumulating market-specific knowledge, all economic actors work on a common ground. This was the case in the E-market: to some extent, individuals' accumulated knowledge (human capital) was almost equivalent to others as the new GPT has not yet undergone a specification process to render more sophisticated designs in technological knowledge. In other words, at the beginning of the GPT's diffusion process only a few actors have accumulated technology-specific knowledge. Technology is new for everyone not having consolidated in usage, no first-mover advantages could have been accumulated conclusively. Hence, all actors face more or less the same terms to start a business: Software developers would simply use their skills to program web sites, while software users (E-commerce entrepreneurs) might not be able to do so. The latter, instead, may have advantageous knowledge such as knowing a business from the "Old Economy". Software integrators would help implementation, internet service providers (ISPs) and application service providers (ASPs) – as these new jobs are termed – assist the incremental innovation process. Many more jobs are created, each contributing a tiny bit to put together an E-business to transform accumulated knowledge out of the "Old Economy" into an innovative "New Economy" firm.

The more the new GPT (the internet) gradually finds its application, and the more the technology's potential is exploited, the higher the complexity of the more specified technology gets. And along with it, the usage of the technology becomes more and more demanding in terms of actors' cognitive capabilities. Consumers also specify their demand, which becomes more and more sophisticated, so that it is not enough any longer to simply program web pages. Integrated solutions are demanded and therefore will be offered. The more entrepreneurs (firms) undergo a learning-by-doing and learning-by-using process, the more technology- and business-specific knowledge is accumulated. During this process the discrepancy in the stock of knowledge between incumbent firms and potential entrepreneurs keeps on growing so that the general terms to start a business within a gradually established market are getting worse while barriers to entry grow. In addition, the turbulence of an emerging market with actors who face a fierce shake-out process might temporarily smother entrepreneurial behavior. Moreover, the increasing complexity of knowledge, the increasing sophistication of technology, inhibits its diffusion among actors. The tacitness of knowledge and actors' absorptive capacities thus decrease the chances of innovation, i.e. the chances to found a firm.[2]

7.2 Modelling Indications

Part I of this work delivers a collection of the intuition on entrepreneurship. Furthermore, it addresses methodological problems and explains how the disappearance of the entrepreneur in economic theory came along. By consolidating the critique of Schumpeter, the body of thought from the Austrian School and Kirzner's adaptations to the entrepreneurial case, it turns out that research on entrepreneurship becomes the pivotal point of a micro-based evolutionary theory. Part II discusses how in general such a heterodox, evolutionary approach ought to look like. Figure 6.1 summarizes the results. Now, it is time to flesh out those ideas with a model to be developed in this part. We start at the micro level modelling heterogeneous actors differing in their individual endowments. Information is incomplete, in particular with respect to the future economic development, saying that agents have to deal with true uncertainty. As a consequence, the bounded rational[3] agents are limited in their cognitive capabilities when perceiving and processing the accumulated information. With regard to novelty, in case agents want to go entrepreneurial, optimal behavior becomes an illusion. Therefore, individuals decide best to their knowledge. Agents form expectations about various conditions of their environment. First, they have to evaluate their individual endowment of resources, capabilities and competencies. Second, they have to reflect on the possibilities to acquire missing complementarities (to be specified later on). And third, they have to assess the "economic situation", i.e. potential profit opportunities.

Figure 7.1 is meant to summarize the basics necessary to start the entrepreneurship model. It combines the methodological ideas discussed and illustrated in figure 6.1 on page 65. In addition, the graph theoretic approach is visualized in this figure referring to the system approach discussed in section 6.2.

The left column in figure 7.1 shows bounded rational agents, who – explicitly considered – show a quasi-random behavior concerning entrepreneurial actions. To concretize the actors' psychology, the fundamental elements of human psychology are characterized (section 8.1.1). Actors have to understand their environment and economic processes, in particular if they intend to undertake entrepreneurial actions. A Schumpeterian entrepreneur, who actualizes *new combinations*, first has to understand the functioning of a new technology (GPT)[4] such as "how the internet works" before he comes up with an innovative business idea.

Thereby, the diffusion of knowledge is an indeterministic process. It depends on social interaction and the agents' learning capabilities. Section 8.1.1 discusses the preparatory work delivered by cognitive psychology. The diffusion of knowledge is modelled using percolation theory.

The understanding of technology is only one part of the story; it is a rather static process in terms of economic change: understanding does not necessarily entail economic action. Actors have to evaluate economic opportunities, they have to evaluate a technology's economic applicability, the question whether there will be a market or not. The social context thereby plays an important role. If many other agents are convinced of some subject matter, one is more tempted to share that opinion. If many agents believe that going entrepreneurial pays, it might stimulate entrepreneurial actions of oneself.

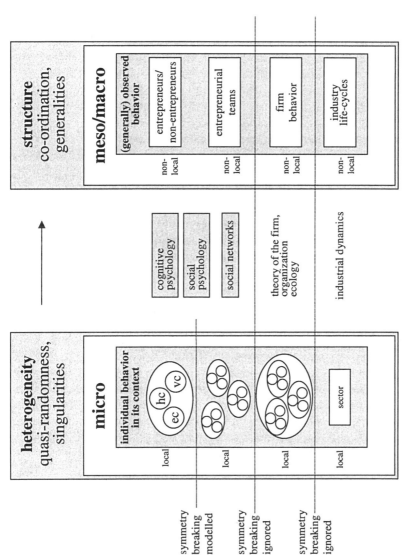

Figure 7.1: The basic building blocks.

Those phenomena are discussed in subsection 8.1.2 by social psychology, which illustrates symmetry-breaking in human behavior. However, the reader has to wait until chapter 9 to see the resulting concept of shared mental models to be implemented into the model.

Then, after understanding technology and evaluating business opportunities, actors will start to engage in a networking process to find support for potential entrepreneurial actions. This will be done in section 8.3. But before that, section 8.2 describes actors from an entrepreneurial perspective. Their *endowment set* is defined by choosing personal characteristics which have been empirically tested many times, and seem to be most eligible to explain an individual's propensity to undertake entrepreneurial actions from an isolated perspective. This small excursion is necessary to merge the methodological approach with the entrepreneurship literature and, moreover, the idea of the network approach in section 8.3 gets clearer. The latter will be modelled via a cellular automaton. Up to that point, the micro level as the focus of entrepreneurial behavior is discussed.

Chapter 9 contains the actual model. Since the methodological discussion advocates a holistic approach to take into account relevant reciprocities, the model contains some modules which have not been discussed explicitly before. The reason for that is simple, as those modules are not the focus of this project. To take into account reciprocities, the macro context of economic actors must not be neglected, since the economy is part of the partially self-created reality. Consequently, the performance of firms within an industry has to be considered. By their performance, firms produce economic indicators. And again, it has to be emphasized explicitly that it is not the intention to explain firm behavior, which might be tempting to think when looking at the model. Therefore, a rather static perspective on firms is taken: exit (survival) depends on an ill-(well-)balanced endowment set constituted by the founders. Competition is substantiated using an oligopoly approach. Hence, on the meso level we end up with a population perspective, and the firm's cost structure as the selection criterion to pay tribute to some stylized facts of an industry's life cycle.

Let us return to figure 7.1 and take a look at the right column. Although we model heterogeneous actors with quasi-random behavior in terms of entrepreneurial actions, we observe actors who found firms and actors who do not found firms, actors we might want to call entrepreneurs and non-entrepreneurs, respectively. Moreover, we will also observe successful and unsuccessful firms, whereby it has to be conceded that a firm's failure originates in the actors' fallible decision in founding an expectedly successful firm. In other words, symmetry-breaking or the adaptability of firms within the competitive process is ignored. So are the specificities of a sector's dynamic evolution.

Chapter 9 is closed by discussing results and some first, modest steps towards an empirical application.

Notes

[1]Compare Bresnahan and Trajtenberg (1995) and Helpman (1998).

[2]The example of the Knowledge-based Economy simply serves for intuitive purposes. Taking a closer look at the short exposition and mapping its argumentation with the adequate literature, we will find in the literature on industry life cycles a lot of such examples. Klepper (1997), Jovanovic and MacDonald (1994), Klepper and Graddy (1990), Gort and Klepper (1982), Abernathy and Utterback (1978) deliver a lot of similar examples which may serve as an example as well. Nevertheless, the example of the Knowledge-based Economy is chosen, since it highlights the role of knowledge diffusion within the process of entrepreneurial behavior.

[3]See e.g. Simon and Egidi (1992) for this discussion.

[4]See example of the Knowledge-based Economy in section 7.1 for explanation.

8 The *Homo agens* in a Socio-Economic Context

8.1 The Cognition Process from a Psychological Perspective

Having figure 7.1 in mind when building a model on entrepreneurial behavior, we start with a set of actors. They neither have complete information/foresight nor perfect (cognitive) capabilities, i.e. we have bounded rational[1] decision-making agents. They cannot make optimal decisions. Decisions are dependent on their knowledge and the information they have or receive, respectively, from their social, political and economic environment.[2] The agents' perception of their environment is thereby contingent to their limited information processing capacity and their limited attentiveness. They have to be selective in their information collection process subject to bounded cognitive capabilities, which, finally results in trial-and-error behavior.[3] Thus, the individual agent becomes a "creative observer" of his socio-economic environment. The latter influences the actor's perception and knowledge of economic "reality" as well as the actor himself creates economic reality within a social cognitive process that directs economic behavior.

8.1.1 Determinants of Human Behavior in a Static Environment, Knowledge Diffusion and Understanding New Technology

Cognitive psychology[4] delivers preparatory work about the role of information in the human decision and cognition process to model economic behavior form the lowest level possible. In contrast to *behaviorism*, which reduces human behavior to a passive *stimulus–reaction* process, cognitive psychology tries to identify the mental process of a thinking agent, who takes an active part acting on the information received.[5] Individuals collect, memorize and use the information about their environment to direct behavior, they learn in order to adjust their behavior.[6] Compared to animals, human beings' cognition capabilities detach their behavior from simple genetically given programs; henceforth, adjustment processes have by far a larger scope. Therefore, the learning process via observation and cognition takes a dominant role in the human decision-making process.[7] It is obvious that not all information, hypothetically available, will be taken into account by the agent, subject to bounded rationality. Besides a limited attention potential and bounded cognitive capabilities, the agent might collect all relevant information due to high (opportunity) costs. There is a need for selectiveness in the information gathering process. Thereby, the search heuristic is guided by former cognition processes which build up certain patterns of (re)cognition.[8] More precisely, if, for example, an individual wants to engage into the stock market, he collects the data he thinks to be relevant for his investment decision.[9] Possible recognition patterns might be looking at fundamental data (i.e. balance sheets) or applying chart analysis techniques. Which pattern the individual chooses, thereby, is a cumulative result of experiences, of former learning processes that make him think to use the right model. The recognition pattern guides the search, and the experience (learning process) influences the recognition pattern. Nevertheless, even having decided to be a "fundamentalist decision maker" in stock market transactions, the individual might not collect and use all the information he has access to. Too many options of a multitude of purchaseable stocks to consider would overflow his limited processing capacity. He has to decide to take just a bit of the data such as profit, a firm's sales growth rate and employment figures.[10] At the same time, the information gathered is categorized in order to cope with its abundance and to obtain a reductionist, distinctive mental representation of an object (profitable stock, non-profitable stock). As already mentioned above, the recognition patterns change over time once the agent realizes that his cognition process leads to false conclusions and decisions. The agents' mental models[11], guides behavior and, at the same time, behavioral consequences influence their mental models. This way, we have individuals that act aim-oriented and therefore make rational decisions best to their knowledge. The latter constitutes individuals' subjective mental model of reality. Conclusively, agents' decisions are subject to error and thus a sustaining cognitive learning process is going on.

When we expand the ideas of cognitive psychology and focus on learning, Piaget (1974) gives a well-structured concept of such a process.[12] According to Piaget, the cognition process is constructivistic and can be categorized into four sub-processes: *assimilation*, *perturbation*, *accommodation* and *equilibration*. *Assimilation* is the cognition process in which the individual integrates the perceived reality in his cognitive system. It is the way how the individual treats incoming novelty. New information is linked to the existing stock of knowledge, to existing mental structures. Some of the new information might not be easy to assimilate and *perturbation* occurs. The cognitive balance is disturbed.[13] Novel information can be surprising or expected, it can be enjoyable or annoying. Once, the individual considers the piece of information to be relevant, he adjusts his pattern of perception and, consequently, his behavior. Hence, *accommodation* takes place in order to reach a psycho-social and cognitive balance, which Piaget calls *equilibration*. This implies that knowledge and rationality are subjective.[14]

Learning is also a major topic in economics. There is a multitude of theories about learning. Brenner (1999) systemized the literature and discussed learning from an economic perspective. Here, it is not the intention to discuss all facets of learning. As mentioned, the issue of entrepreneurship behavior raises methodological issues, therefore, the focus is put on how to model a learning process on a very rudimentary basis. Suffice it to refer to the relevant literature, which also favors a psychological approach as the apparently most promising one.[15] For the purpose of modelling, some adaptations and simplifications will be made in the following.

Knowledge and its Diffusion – the Catalyst of Economic Behavior

It was stated that the human mind is taken as a ontological foundation of modelling economic phenomena. Conclusively, the cognition process becomes the crucial element to model specific economic behaviors. And with bounded rational actors, therefore, knowledge becomes the source of human action. Hence, knowledge becomes also the decisive determinant within the innovation process which the entrepreneur is the driving force of. In economic theory, however, it turns out to be a difficult task to take into account all nuances of knowledge.

Referring to a perfect rationality postulate, it is a contradiction to talk about any kind of imperfect knowledge at all. On the contrary, heterodox approaches still try hard to model knowledge in its nature. Knowledge has been neglected for a long time when modelling economic processes. The first who integrated the notion of knowledge into the economic process was Arrow (1962b). He models the incentive to innovate, i.e. to generate new knowledge, considering market structure. But when it comes to the specificities of knowledge he circumvent the issue of the public goods characteristics of knowledge in order to avoid so-called technological *spillovers*. Assuming perfect patenting, the appropriability of innovation rents is guaranteed. Similarly, Non-Tournament models by Dasgupta and Stiglitz are built on the assumption that "(...) *knowledge is monopolised by a firm when it pays for it.*"[16] Thus, knowledge is treated as an ordinary private good, which does not differ much from other input factors (land, real capital, etc.). Levin and Reiss (1984) first allow for technological *spillovers* into a Dasgupta/Stiglitz-type model to pay tribute that knowledge does neither wear out nor is rival in multiple usage.

But taking into account the role of knowledge (in the way cognitive psychology does) as the fuel and the outcome of a complex cognition process which eventually guides the behavior of a *Homo agens*, an economic man acting best to his knowledge, we have to make some more differentiations, irrespective of a definition of knowledge to put into practice in an economic model.[17]

The Austrian School provides a lot of contributions to knowledge, originating from the criticism on equilibrium analysis.[18] Nonetheless, for modelling purposes only some selected literature will be used. Polanyi (1958) introduces *tacit knowledge* what Berry (1997) similarly paraphrases *implicit learning*, the sort of knowledge we know we have but cannot articulate. Arrow (1962a) coins the concept of *learning by doing* and Rosenberg (1982) specified *learning by using*. Lundvall (1998) makes the useful distinction between information and knowledge; and Lundvall and Johnson (1994) reflect on *the learning economy*. Information would manifest the knowledge which can be transmitted via any kind of information technologies, whereas knowledge would imply a learning process to, first, understand the existing stock of knowledge and, second, adds further knowledge to the stock of knowledge.

The literature on the Knowledge-based Theory of the Firm also shifted its emphasis to the role of knowledge and capabilities. Penrose (1959a) considers the firm as a *collection of resources* that seizes its *productive opportunities* given a certain endowment of human and real capital subject to available capabilities.[19] Eliasson (1990) substantiated such competence as *receiver competence*, i.e. the firm's capability to acquire external (technological) knowledge and economic opportunities. The former Cohen and Levinthal (1989) specified as a firm's *absorptive capacity*, which basically means the capacity to understand new technologies necessary in order to make economic use of them.[20]

As the focus is chosen to be on individual actors, only some aspects will be selected to model entrepreneurial behavior. Bounded rational actors all have a certain understanding of the existing stock of knowledge, contingent to their individual cognitive capabilities and experiences. It is the result of a cumulative, lifelong learning process. Some of the knowledge acquired will be codified; some will be tacit, which an actor implicitly learned by experience and social interaction. As a consequence, the individual's cognitive capabilities are also a determinant of the diffusion of knowledge. Concerning the emission of knowledge, the actor transmits

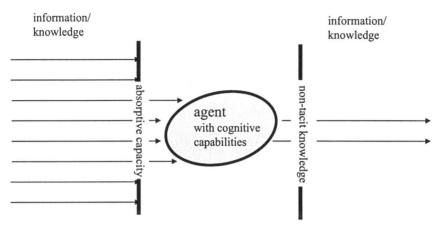

Figure 8.1: The diffusion of information/knowledge with bounded rational actors.

information and codified knowledge, provided that he is willing to do so. The rest of knowledge remains to the actor's *human embodied knowledge capital*.[21] The total of an actor's knowledge will be called human capital in the model below. Evidently, information will spread more rapidly among actors than knowledge that requires a learning process. Thereby, the distance of actors has also an impact of the diffusion of knowledge. Information might diffuse with zero marginal cost; *sticky knowledge*, as von Hippel (1994) calls it, is effectively transferred via a frequent, face-to-face contact and, furthermore, depends on its regional context.[22] The diffusion of knowledge is not only restricted by the cognitive capabilities and the (observable) behavior which limits the emission of an actor's knowledge but also it is dependent on the *absorptive* cognitive capacity to receive, absorb and use external knowledge,[23] knowledge that spills over from others.

Figure 8.1 sketches the basic elements required to simplify the knowledge diffusion process given a bounded rational actor with a certain degree of absorptive capacity and knowledge transmission, constrained by the tacitness of knowledge. There is one concession made: technically, the actor serves as a valve that regulates (technological) knowledge transfer via actors, illustrating the duality of spillovers – absorption and emission. The generation of new knowledge is neglected at this point but will be addressed in the final model in which the shared mental model, the founding threshold,[24] reflects the dynamic process of knowledge creation.

Without knowledge diffusing through society, no economic change would happen. Without knowledge about new inventions and new technology, no entrepreneurs would arise out of society. The diffusion of knowledge, how-

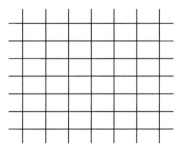

Figure 8.2: The square lattice.

ever, is neither a deterministic process, nor a negligible aspect to be denied by a perfect rationality postulate. Knowledge is necessary to activate actors, to initiate entrepreneurial behavior. Furthermore, to pay tribute to the role of indeterminism discussed in the previous part and model an indeterministic diffusion process, percolation theory will be used for two reasons, to give a metaphor and to incorporate this indeterministic process into the entrepreneurship model later on.

Modelling Knowledge Diffusion with Percolation Theory

The research field of percolation theory has a history of over forty years and has become more and more popular in various scientific disciplines. Percolation theory deals with *disordered* phenomena.[25] It tries to describe the flow of fluids through medium, the spreading of epidemics or forest fires and so forth. More precisely, it investigates the *topology* and the *"(...) interconnectedness of microscopic elements of (...) [a] system."*[26] It pictures a system's apparently random morphology, which eludes a deterministic description – at least on a micro-level – forborne by quantum theory. *"Percolation theory tells us when a system is* macroscopically *open to a given phenomenon."*[27] For example, it tells us the condition when a filter bag is penetrable by coffee. A filter without pores does not allow coffee to trickle through (percolate) into the can. The more pores, the more likely a closed system becomes an open system that shows a flow. The threshold that marks the transition from a closed to an open system is called *percolation threshold*.[28]

To illustrate percolation processes, a regular network illustrated by a square lattice shown in figure 8.2 is used.[29]

Looking at the squares of the lattice, we talk of *sites*. Regarding the edge of a square, we talk of *bonds*. Hence, there are two percolation problems, the *site percolation* and the *bond percolation problem*. Taking the latter first: the bonds are either *occupied*, i.e. open to flow or diffusion, or *vacant*, that is impenetrable. The probability p gives the likelihood that a bond is occupied (open) or vacant (closed). Conclusively, two sites, the location of two crossing lines in case of *bond percolation*, are connected if there is at least one path of bonds that connects two sites (intersections). If $p = 1$, then all sites are *connected* with each other. A set of sites, isolated to other sites by vacant bonds, builds a *cluster*. The transition point, which discriminates a *macroscopically* closed from an open structure, is called the *bond percolation threshold*.

When considering *site percolation*, a site is either occupied with probability p or vacant with probability *1-p*. Two neighboring sites are connected, if both of them are occupied. *Site percolation* occurs, if there is an infinite[30] *sample-spanning cluster* of occupied sites. Analyzing the square lattice, the value of the percolation threshold, p_{cb} in the case of bond percolation and p_{cs} in the case of site percolation, is equal to $1/2$ and 0.5927, respectively.

Sahimi (1994) summarizes the *topological properties* concerning some important quantities as follows:

(i) *Percolation probability P(p)*. This is the probability that, when the fraction of occupied bonds is p, a given site belongs to the infinite (sample-spanning) cluster of occupied bonds.

(ii) Accessible fraction $X^A(p)$. This is that fraction of occupied bonds belonging to the infinite cluster.

(iii) Backbone fraction $X^B(p)$. This is the fraction of occupied bonds in the infinite cluster which actually carry flow or current, since some of the bonds in the cluster are dead-end and do not carry any flow. The backbone of a percolating system plays a fundamental role in its transport properties, because the tortuosity of the transport paths is controlled by the structure of the backbone.

(iv) *Correlation length $\xi_p(p)$*. This is the typical radius of the connected clusters for $p < p_c$, and the length scale over which the random network is macroscopically homogeneous (i.e., the length scale over which the properties of the system are independent of its linear size L for $p > p_c$). Thus, in any Monte Carlo simulations of percolation we must have $L >> \xi_p$ for the results to be independent of L.

(v) *Average number of clusters of size s (per lattice site)* $n_s(p)$, since sn_s is the probability that a given site is part of an s-cluster, a mean cluster size $S_p(p)$ can be defined by

$$S_p(p) = \frac{\sum_s s^2 n_s}{\sum_s s n_s} \qquad (8.1)$$

(vi) *Effective electrical conductivity* g_e. This is the electrical conductivity of a random resistor network in which a fraction p of bonds are conducting and the rest are insulating. Similarly, if a network represents the pore space of a porous medium in which a fraction p of the pores are open to flow or diffusion, an effective diffusivity D_e and a hydrodynamic permeability k can also be defined.

(vii) *Effective elastic moduli G*. These are the elastic moduli of the network in which a fraction p of the bonds are elastic elements (e.g., springs), while the rest have no rigidity of stiffness (i.e., they are cut).[31]

Figure 8.3 illustrates some of the characteristics of site percolation in a square lattice depending on the probability p. $X^I(p)$ depicts the fraction of isolated occupied sites. The analogy to economic phenomena is straightforward. Concerning the diffusion of knowledge, the *percolation probability P(p)* denotes the probability that economic agents (sites) belong to the infinite or sample-spanning[32] cluster that perceives and understands the diffusing new technological knowledge. $X^A(p)$ is the actual *accessible fraction* of economic agents that belong to the infinite cluster, i.e. to the economic agents that receive and understand the incoming knowledge. The *backbone fraction* $X^B(p)$ is the part of the knowledge-receiving agents that carry the flow of knowledge, whereas some of the agents are dead-end and do not carry any flow; knowledge remains tacit. The *correlation length* ξ_p can be interpreted as the regional aspect of knowledge diffusion, thinking of local innovation systems (clusters) and taking into account the locality of external economies of scale that will also have an impact on the mean cluster size $S_p(p)$. Furthermore, the *effective electrical conductivity* g_e can be equated with the effective diffusivity of a set of actors with knowledge. Thereby, it has to take care of the different kinds of knowledge: The diffusivity of pure information will be high but the more complex knowledge gets, the more absorptive capacities and limiting spillovers (owing to the tacitness of knowledge) become inhibiting elements of knowledge diffusion.

To visualize the idea of percolation, figure 8.4 shows three diagrams indicating different states of a medium's permeability. The underlying program source is given in appendix B.1.

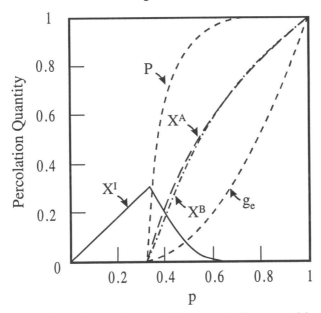

Figure 8.3: The dependence of some of the percolation quantities on p, the fraction of occupied sites, in site percolation on a simple cubic lattice.

Source: Sahimi (1994, p. 13). Copyright © 1994. Reprinted by permission of Taylor & Francis.

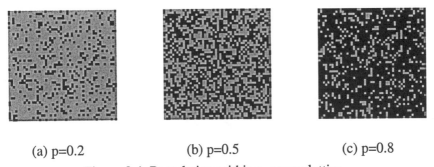

(a) p=0.2   (b) p=0.5   (c) p=0.8

Figure 8.4: Percolation within a square lattice.

The percolation probability p gives the fraction of occupied (permeable) sites within a square lattice of n^2 actors. Gray squares signify vacant (non-permeable) sites and black squares occupied ones. In case (a), the percolation probability is $p = 0.2$, i.e. a low fraction of occupied sites, so that the existence of a sample-spanning cluster is very unlikely; as a result, more isolated clusters[33] occur. As p increases, the probability of percolation grows. At the percolation threshold, which is about $p=0.5$, the fraction of occupied sites that belong to the sample-spanning cluster rapidly increases as diagram (b) shows (compare also figure 8.3). With $p=0.8$, almost all occupied sites are part of that cluster, meaning that almost every occupied site of the lattice is reachable.

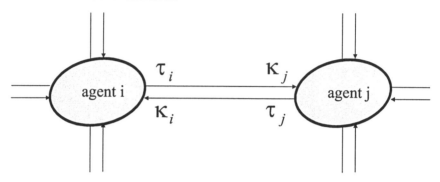

Figure 8.5: Actors within a lattice.

τ = transferable (non-tacit) knowledge emitted by agent i,j.
κ = absorptive capacity of agent i,j.

Now, the notion of percolation theory will serve as a tool to model the diffusion of knowledge. According to figure 8.1, the agents have been idealized by their individual absorptive capacities. Furthermore, knowledge has been differentiated by its tacitness. Putting together figure 8.1 and figure 8.2 yields figure 8.5: we obtain a set of actors scattered over a square lattice. Information is emitted and received by actors. Apart from the absorptive capacity κ of the agent, which determines whether the incoming knowledge will be understood or not, the quantity τ of transferrable (non-tacit) knowledge will be emitted by the agent.

For convenience, the actors have to be considered as an occupied site and the connections determine the permeability of the medium, i.e. the diffusivity of the set of actors thinking of knowledge diffusion.

In a next step, knowledge is differentiated further to take into account the heterogeneity of bounded rational actors according to their absorptive capacities.

The Diffusion of Knowledge with Bounded Rational Agents, Having Different States of Absorptive Capacities and States of Tacitness

Notice that the role of knowledge is to be emphasized for several reasons: (a) to refrain from the *Homo economicus*, the perfect rationality postulate has to be dropped as mentioned in the chapters above. Subsequently, because of the heterogeneity of actors and their having different endowments in capabilities, knowledge has (b) to be discussed from a methodological perspective; therefore, graph theory, a less restrictive apparatus than the one used in equilibrium analysis, was introduced to model economic behavior. Moreover, since the ultimate focus of this project still is the investigation of entrepreneurial behavior, (c) the role of knowledge within the entrepreneurial process, within the innovation process has to be taken even more into account; the entrepreneurial function, as Schumpeter stated, originates in carrying out innovations, *new combinations* which imply newly generated knowledge. He differentiated *invention* from *innovation*.[34] Innovation signifies the actualization of an invention, of new knowledge. In order for the entrepreneur to be able to innovate, knowledge – created by invention – has first to be available, and second, understood by actors. No matter whether the entrepreneur himself or another person generates new knowledge, without new knowledge entrepreneurial behavior comes to a halt. Apart from that, there is a further reason (e) which brings us back to the intuitive example in section 7.1. The Knowledge-based Economy in the 1990s highlights the role of knowledge in economy as well as delivering a unique example for an entrepreneurial economy.

Now, for the purpose of implementing knowledge into the entrepreneurial model below, knowledge diffusion, taking into account tacitness and absorptive capacities, will be modelled by using a percolation model.

Figure 8.6: Percolation – agents with heterogeneous absorptive capacities.

A square lattice is considered in which each square denotes an actor with a given level of absorptive capacity (figure 8.6). The program is given in appendix B.4. Each rectangle represents a certain point in time, the starting point is top left. The changing colors of squares illustrate the five different stages of knowledge being inherent to actors. Absorptive capacities are not visualized but randomly distributed via agents.[35] Equation 8.2 shows the tuple of an actor i with a stock of knowledge w and absorptive capacities κ_i:

$$a_i = \{w_i, \kappa_i\} \tag{8.2}$$

In the top left lattice of figure 8.6, we see that only a few actors have a certain stock of knowledge. Dark squares signify actors without this kind of knowledge. A light gray square represents actor i with a stock of knowledge, $w_{\kappa_i} = 1$, that has sufficient absorptive capacities to process the new incoming knowledge: the basics of a yet unspecified GPT are understood. Interaction is modelled by using a cellular (von Neumann-)automaton, and knowledge propagates through agents subject to their absorptive capacities. In the second lattice, for example, some of the light gray clusters enclose a dark gray square, i.e. this signifies an actor with higher absorptive capacities who is able to absorb more of the incoming information than the surrounding others. In each time step, while knowledge is diffusing, actors learn about e.g. a new technology. And the darker a square gets, the higher the agents' absorptive capacities are and the more the actors are able to use technological knowledge of a higher level of sophistication. In the lattice bottom right, all agents have partially absorbed the diffusing knowledge; the dark gray color at the beginning, in the lattice top left, vanished completely, saying that all actors absorbed the basic understanding of the new technology such as how the internet works and how to use it. The highest possible level of knowledge, $w_{\kappa_i} = 4$, is scarcely reached; the last lattice shows that black squares only occur sporadically. To put it differently, all agents understand the basics of the knowledge trickling through, but as soon as the complexity of a technology increases, the usage of such will be constrained by the individuals absorptive capacities, the tacitness of knowledge, the connectiveness of agents and the randomness of the time-dependent diffusion process.

What Can We Learn from Percolation Theory?

Considering the lowest level of knowledge complexity, $w_{\kappa_i} = 1$ (figure 8.3), the percolation probability is equal to $P_{(p)} = 1$, hence percolation has occurred. All agents perceived the new technology and have a low-level understanding of it. With increasing usage, technology becomes more sophisticated denying more and more actors intellectual access. Hence, percolation becomes less likely. In the extreme case of $w_{\kappa_i} = 4$, percolation is even impossible. Table 8.1 indicates the distribution of absorptive capacities among actors. Absorptive capacities are assumed to be binomially distributed. All actors have a certain level of absorptive capacities κ. The probability of either having absorptive capacities $\kappa \in \{1,2,3,4\}$, respectively, is a binomial distribution with $n=3$ and $p=0.5$.

κ_i	0	1	2	3	4
$p = \kappa$	0	0.125	0.375	0.375	0.125
$p > \kappa$	1	0.875	0.5	0.125	0

Table 8.1: Distribution of absorptive capacities.

Using figure 8.3 in order to interpret table 8.1, we see that for $\kappa = 1$ or $\kappa = 2$ the percolation threshold is reached. Almost all actors belong to the sample-spanning cluster, i.e. almost all actors perceive and process the incoming knowledge constrained by their absorptive capacities κ. To that extent, all actors understand technology and realize its potential. As the GPT gets more elaborated by usage and market coordination and the diffusion of knowledge gets higher in complexity, the percolation threshold might not be reached and the fraction of actors not able to process the technological knowledge is high.[36]

Besides the connectivity (reachability) of actors, the dynamics of the diffusing knowledge also looks different when looking at each complexity level. Figure 8.7 shows the corresponding diffusion curves of the four different knowledge complexity levels $w \in \{1,2,3,4\}$, as pictured in figure 8.6. The more complex the diffusing knowledge is, the longer the diffusion process takes. Accordingly, the fraction of actors who perceive and understand the incoming knowledge decreases reciprocally with complexity.

To summarize: The cognition process of bounded rational actors has been investigated. Knowledge has been stressed as the fundamental determinant of human (economic) action. In particular, when referring to entrepreneurial actions, the generation of innovative knowledge is critical. In order for the potential of new technologies to unfold, the technology has to be cognitively processed by actors. The easiness to grasp technology thereby decides whether a swarm of innovations occurs or not. Looking at it from the actors' perspective, their absorptive capacities are the limiting factors and inhibit the diffusivity of knowledge.

So far, the agents modelled above are still passive and receptive. Whether knowledge is accumulated depends merely on a given, individual, cognitive profile. Yet, no economic action has been performed. All we talked about was the process of recognition, the process of learning about new technologies. The fact of understanding, however, does not imply a deterministic behavior just by itself. Understanding technology is only one part

# of actors

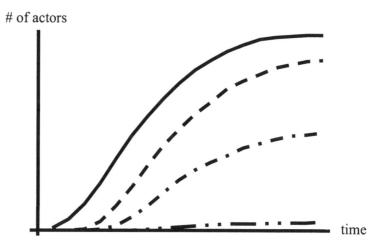

Figure 8.7: The dynamics of knowledge diffusion.

of the story, the motivation to actually use new technology (knowledge) is another. The process of innovation by entrepreneurs, the application of technological knowledge, depends on the alleged demand, the subjective utility expressed by prospective consumers. The economic potential has first to be assessed by actors to arouse their motivation to act. This evaluation is a subjective process by a potential entrepreneur. It is not an optimization problem to simply discount future innovation rents and equating with the costs of innovation. Ex ante, objectivity is an illusion prevented by epistemological reservations (Arrow (1991)). Economic reality is the result of human interaction, hence, a self-creating process motivated by economic actors. Therefore, successful, entrepreneurial actions are the outcome of a well-anticipated commonality of economic behavior. The entrepreneur excels as a splendid (creative) observer, who on top of it manages to take a major part in the creation of economic reality.

To bring in the dynamics of purposeful (inter-)acting agents, the process of the evolution of economic prospects in a social context is discussed in the next section. Eventually, the evolution of new firms and sectors, spurred by the individual actor's behavior will be elaborated.

8.1.2 Determinants of Human Behavior in a Dynamic Environment – Perception, Creation and Evaluation of New Technological Potentials

So far, we have considered the cognitive process of a bounded rational agent in a static context. Agents learn about their technological and economic environment, so that an adjustment in behavior may be induced. But, considering learning within the economic process, we have to take into account a dynamic environment.

Learning to ride a bike is different from learning within the economic process, especially with regard to entrepreneurial behavior. The former describes a learning process by given facts: the aspiring candidate, who wants to learn how to ride a bike, has to cope with given facts of nature, with irrevocable natural laws that constitute reality.[37] The economic reality, however, is different. Economic behavior means subjective perception and social interaction. Actors recognize their economic environment but, on the other hand, they create their economic reality since they take part in the economic process by being consumer, producer or entrepreneur, respectively.[38] With social interaction, we obtain a reciprocity of the agent as an observer and a creator of reality. Actors adjust their behavior to their mental model about real economic processes. Doing this, they influence the mental model of others who assimilate this change of the dynamic environment to finally adjust their own behavior. In conclusion, economic behavior goes beyond mere stimulus–reaction behavior and even more beyond simple adjustment processes to synchronize one's mental model with reality; the economic agent, the learning individual as an observer of the economic reality, takes an active part in creating economic reality itself. Thereby, the most influential agent in this creative process may be considered to be the entrepreneur.

In the last section, we discussed the cognition process of agents. While they learn about new technologies and obtain new knowledge, economic behavior might be adjusted, provided the actor senses a cognitive dissonance. Thus, the environment has an impact on economic behavior. This influence, however, is not a unilateral one. Economic behavior is no persistent law of nature – though this seems to be true for some basic patterns of economic behavior, because every agent adjusts behavior to the economic sphere which he himself is a part of (bimodal ontology). The social context influences economic behavior as much as economic behavior influences economic reality. To incorporate those aspects, the findings of social psychology will be discussed briefly.

Social psychology puts the human cognition process into a social context. It studies "*(...) how people think about, influence, and relate to one another.*"[39] Human cognition is not simply a one-way process in adjusting one's behavior to a static environment. The behavior of individual A influences the behavior of another individual B and vice versa, opening up room for strategic and manipulative behavior to twist social and economic reality. The social context is crucial for our behavior. The social surroundings influence our *self-awareness*: in a group, we become self-conscious of our qualities that make us different to other members of the group, such as being a black among white people or being a high-skilled among unskilled workers. *Self-interest* dyes our social judgement attributing the responsibility for certain undesirable events to others, whereas making oneself more responsible for successful ones. The desire to belong to a certain group or at least to leave a certain impression on a group, our *self-concern*, makes us adjust one's behavior in a way that induces a certain social behavior. For instance, politicians try to understand the voters' needs during a campaign to get the majority vote. Without considering the social context of an individual, it seems to be impossible to predict a certain (economic) behavior. Even the individual himself often has a hard time predicting his own behavior.[40] It is not always obvious to the individual what has been influencing his performed behavior. Sometimes, he might not even be able to explain his behavior to others. Nevertheless, the individual's *self-concept* is critical in decision making and performance. His *self-esteem*, his evaluation of his self worth, determines his appraisal of his traits and abilities. Ruvolo and Markus (1992) corroborated the hypothesis that people with a high self-esteem, with a positive appraisal of themselves, outperform others with a rather negative self–appraisal. The optimistic belief in one's competence, effectiveness and actions (*self-efficacy*)[41] renders confidence which yields positive results just by itself. Self-efficacy, however, is improved not simply by self-persuasion but by others who credit one's "outstanding" qualities. As a consequence, mutual appreciation among group members increases their self-efficacy so that the group's collective efficacy, the group's belief in their comprehensive competencies and capabilities, exceeds the sum of the individuals' self-efficacy.[42] As a conclusion, some decisions become more likely to be made as a group decision compared to a decision in isolation. Hence, symmetry breaking in behavior can be observed.[43] Considering the decision to found a firm, such kind of decision requires high self-esteem and self-efficacy, a decision which is more likely to be made as a group.

So far, we discussed the individuals' and contextual determinants of a decision-making process. In the following, we will discuss the phenomenon of the *self-serving bias*, a psychological aspect that reinforces self-efficacy and, consequently, certain behavior.

> *As we process self-relevant information, a potent bias intrudes. We readily excuse our failures, accept credit for our successes, and in many ways see ourselves as better than average. Such self-enhancing perceptions enable most people to enjoy the benefits of high self-esteem, while occasionally suffering the perils of pride.*[44]

Despite inferiority complexes, which seem inherent to all of us,[45] there is evidence to the tendency that we perceive ourselves favorably.[46]

Positive events are attributed to oneself, whereas negative events are attributed to others or to given circumstances.[47] When people evaluate themselves in comparison to others, they rank themselves higher than average in almost any dimension which is *subjective* and *socially desirable*. This phenomenon is even more pronounced when someone compares himself to unknown individuals.[48] Most business managers for example rank their performance higher than their average peer.[49] Similarly, when evaluating future events, Weinstein (1980) detected an *unrealistic optimism about future life events.* Irrespective of the questions individuals were asked, such as future job search, risk of HIV-infection, probability of getting divorced, etc., most evaluated themselves to have better chances to desirable future events than others.[50] Concerning an individual's opinion about what others think, we observe the so-called *false consensus effect*. The extent to which other people agree to one's own opinion tends to be overestimated by individuals.[51] In the same way as people assess their abilities and desirable or successful behaviors, the individual that fails tends to consider his failure to be common to all, such as "accidental" tax evasion. On the contrary, virtues and successful behaviors, he considers to be unique to his person (*false uniqueness effect*).[52]

McClelland (1961)[53] is one of the first who profoundly analyzed the social and cultural context of potential entrepreneurs and thus brings in a social–psychological aspect into the entrepreneurship discussion. He investigated the (social) psychological aspects of *the achieving society* and conjectured a basic motivation, a *need for achievement* within stereotypical societies; societies in which typical, cultural and societal values are transferred via socialization and education, so that as a result, a fundamental tendency towards entrepreneurial behavior becomes evident in society.[54]

8.1.3 Summary

To put the *Homo economicus* into perspective, the cognitive process of bounded rational agents has been illustrated from a psychological perspective. Agents build subjective mental representations of the perceived reality. The subjective mental model in general will correlate with reality[55] but will not be completely consistent with reality, since agents have to learn. Furthermore, mental representations will also differ among actors. Via (social) interaction the mental models' resemblance is coordinated among actors.[56] Thus, we identify fundamental, coordinative forces, which tend to bring in line the (heterogeneous) actors' mental models and the implied behavior. Considering the theoretical hypotheses and the empirical evidence in social psychology, the phenomenon of a common possibly false[57] behavior via reinforcement effects of certain behavior becomes possible. Figure 8.8 illustrates the basic idea of an economic agent that observes and

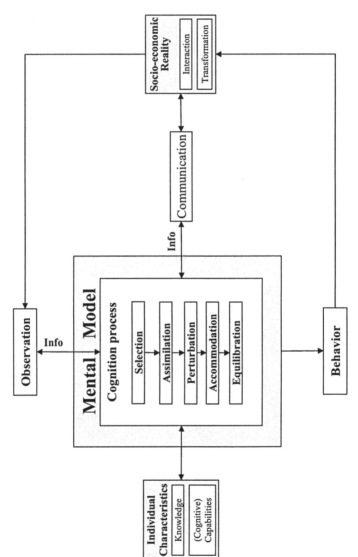

Figure 8.8: The mental model – the agent as a "creative observer".

influences his social and economic environment: the "creative observer". This figure pictures social interaction, i.e. communication[58] and the participation in the economic transformation process. It renders information by experiencing his direct social and economic proximity. The agent processes the information gathered, and the resulting mental model, which in addition is influenced by individual characteristics (accumulated knowledge, capabilities, etc.), determines his behavior, which in return has an effect on (socio-economic) reality. The aspect to be stressed here, is that social interaction affects the interrelated mental models of the individuals involved. And, as individuals act in accordance with their mental model, any change in the model influences the cognition process (attention, perception, etc.) and, hence, results in a certain behavior, which becomes part of reality.

The closer we get to the actual, basic model of entrepreneurial behavior in this work, the more the agent has to be idealized and adapted to the entrepreneurial case. After the cognition process of heterogeneous (bounded rational) agents has been integrated into a socio-economic context, the cornerstone of an interdependent, socio-economic dynamics to model entrepreneurial behavior has almost been accomplished.

For the reader's guidance a reference to figure 7.1 might be helpful. It sketches the author's incremental procedure ensuing to model entrepreneurial behavior. In this figure, the behavior of individuals is the subject of investigation. Considering entrepreneurial behavior, the birth of new firms in particular, meso- and macro phenomena have to be taken into account to describe individual behavior. Furthermore, between the isolated individual level – now, specified by the cognition process as provided by cognitive psychology – and the social context of economic behavior – fleshed out by social psychology – symmetry breaking[59] is considered.

Besides those individual and social psychological aspects, which are common to all bounded rational actors, there are more specific determinants that are found in literature and underpin the specificities of entrepreneurial behavior. Still, two further steps are to be taken to round off the basic setting of such a model: first, the endowment set which seems to be crucial for entrepreneurial behavior from an empirical perspective will be stated, and second, the theory of social networks will serve to substantiate the socio-economic context of human behavior in the model.

8.2 Characterizing the *Homo agens* from an Entrepreneurial Perspective

In the first chapter of this book, the twelve "themes" of the entrepreneurial role elaborated by Hébert and Link (1982) were cited. Afterwards, in section 2.2, those twelve themes were evaluated in terms of their appropriateness to characterize the entrepreneur. Some items were cancelled out because it was argued that the entrepreneurial role cannot be investigated in a static context. Other items addressed the issue of disequilibrium analysis subject to bounded rationality which concerns all economic actors. Kirzner's entrepreneur as an arbitrageur similarly emphasizes the role of information in the market process (in disequilibrium). Knight pointed out that it is especially the entrepreneur who has to deal with uncertainty, with an indeterministic future. Taking uncertainty as a stylized fact, again, all actors have to cope with it. It was Schumpeter who stressed the entrepreneurial role within the innovation process. His entrepreneur, discussed in section 3.4, brings along economic change, he brings along novelty. When we put Schumpeter's entrepreneur in the context outlined above, we obtain a watchful observer of the socio-economic process, who believes in his competence and power to influence economic reality, i.e. to innovate, to found a firm and to make profits.

Entrepreneurial component   In the model below (chapter 9), each actor has – at least to a certain extent – the potential to be a Schumpeterian entrepreneur. Therefore, the first component of an actor is called "entrepreneurial spirit," which can also be interpreted as the actor's propensity to perform entrepreneurial action by his intrinsic motivation.

The entrepreneurial spirit, as it is labelled in this context, has been investigated in many studies. Some personal factors are decisive for entrepreneurial behavior. Szyperski and Nathusius (1977) offer a lot of apparently necessary qualities of firm founders. Klandt (1984) gives a good overview of the traits of firm founders.[60] Several dimensions of personal factors are analyzed such as the *dynamic personality, age, sex,* and so forth. Though most of these personal traits are influential, they are not decisive for entrepreneurial behavior.[61] Klandt (1984) points out that situational factors prevail. And organization ecologists[62] continue in this direction criticizing such trait approaches. Nevertheless, personal factors (entrepreneurial spirit) cannot be neglected. At least, the entrepreneurial element has to be considered as a residual component inherent to the individual actor.

Human capital   With the second component the human capital of an actor is taken into account. The human capital approach, constituted by Theodor W. Schultz[63], and elaborated by Gary S. Becker among others,[64] allows for an empirical application. It tries to explain optimal investment in human capital and delivers insights on income distribution. The theoretical concept basically is derived from investment theory in physical capital using marginal analysis. In the model below, this theory will not be used in its strict, neoclassical sense, but in a less compelling way: it is simply seen as a positive correlation between the actor's human capital and his economic performance. The human capital component is meant to emphasize the necessity of knowledge for any entrepreneurial action. Goebel (1990), Hunsdiek and May-Strobl (1986) for example tested the influence of personal resources on the entrepreneur's success. Despite the mixed results and some doubtful comments on such an approach,[65] a higher-skill level, in particular a higher degree of business specific knowledge of founders, have a positive impact on success.

Since agents are bounded rational, they know about the importance of human capital for establishing a firm, but they do not know the actual return when they decide to do so; when offering their human capital to the labor market, they face a different situation. Therefore, agents decide in a dichotomous way; if they expect the returns[66] of going entrepreneurial be higher than being an employee, they will decide to become an entrepreneur. Moreover, the agents' human capital is assumed to be the crucial productive element for the long-run survival of the firm, once it is founded.

Venture capital   The third element we include into the agents' endowment vector is the component of venture capital. Herewith, we pay tribute to the discussion whether "the roles of the capitalist and the entrepreneur" can be separated. The "early French view" rather saw the entrepreneur as a risk bearer; the "English view" identified the entrepreneur as the capitalist. Schumpeter (1939a) discusses the role of money, too.[67] The bottom line is that potential entrepreneurs need to have capital to start their business, regardless of whether they own it themselves or borrow it from others, according to Evans and Jovanovic (1989) and Evans and Leighton (1989). Empirical evidence supports the hypothesis that entrepreneurs in general face financial and liquidity constraints.[68] Levinthal (1991), furthermore, shows that the initial endowment of a newly established firm increases the probability of survival at the beginning. As the model is meant to be a platform approach to be specified later on for empirical application, a discrimination between several *populations* such as venture and human capitalists is not undertaken.

The intuition we draw out of this discussion is that each agent is endowed with a certain amount of financial capital, which he can spend on a business venture. Again, we do not bother about the details, whether he inherited or accumulated a certain amount of money by saving.

So far, the individual agents are characterized by their endowment factors.[69] Each actor possesses the potential to be an entrepreneur, as von Mises suggests from a theoretic perspective, and – as empirical data shows – most agents have.[70] Thereby, the decision (human action) is not an optimal behavior, calculating what the maximal return to total – human and (free disposable) venture – capital is. Although the long-term survival of a firm once founded is highly dependent on the agent's human capital. As we vested all agents with the option to own venture capital, we can incorporate the notion of risk bearing and uncertainty.[71]

These three components summarize each a category of influential (empirically motivated) determinants for entrepreneurial behavior.[72] An agent might have a certain amount of each component necessary to establish a firm, although he might not have enough of it.

In that case, the agent needs to complete the minimum endowment necessary to his mind, which might be found in one's social network.

8.3 The Sociological Context of Actors

8.3.1 Theory of Social Networks

In the previous sections, the context of human (economic) behavior was gradually introduced and the entrepreneurial specificities of actors stated. The section about cognitive psychology illustrated the determinants of knowledge diffusion; the section on social psychology went beyond the mere, technical understanding of real-world aspects and addressed the social context and its influence on agents' evaluation of future economic developments and their subsequent behavior which, thus, results in a partially self-fulfilling process. Both, the diffusion of knowledge as well as the common evaluation of economic opportunities are substantiated by socio-economic interaction. Social network theory will help us now to bring in the dynamics of human behavior in its social context. Thereby, we also manage to climb up the aggregation level within the model.

Wasserman and Faust (1994) summarize the basic assumptions about actors, relations and structure when doing social network analysis as follows:

- *Actors and their actions are viewed as interdependent rather than independent, autonomous units.*
- *Relational ties (linkages) between actors are channels for transfer or "flow" of resources (either material like money, or nonmaterial, like information, political support, friendship, or respect).*
- *Network models focusing on individuals view the network structural environment as providing opportunities for or constraints on individual action.*

• *Network models conceptualize structure (whether social, economic, political, and so forth) as enduring patterns of relations among actors.*[73]

Considering the birth of new firms, the entrepreneurial process strongly depends on such aspects. Once actors understand technology and commonly assume a high economic potential, future potential entrepreneurs might need their social network to complete the initial endowment, which is presumed to be necessary to start a business. They have to figure out how to get access to required resources[74] and whether the necessary competence to combine these resources[75] is available. Some of the resources and competencies can be inherent to the agent, others have to be acquired on the market (Coase (1988)). Since it is not argued on the firm level[76] following Birley (1985), the *pre-organization* phase is to be investigated in order to stress the importance of an agent's social network as a main source of help to obtain resources and competencies to start a business.

Granovetter (1973) provided the pioneering work on social networks. Actors' interactions constitute the economic process. Social network theory investigates the relations, the "*ties*" between those actors.[77] Relations may have several causal motivations. Actors exchange goods or services, or simply information, they transfer attitudes and norms, and build expectations. Thus they have a mutual influence on each other; an aspect which has already been covered above. The ties between actors are either strengthened or loosened by the level, frequency and already existing reciprocity of their relationship. The *role-set*[78] is constituted by direct relations between actors. Such relations will put more pressure on one's behavior than indirect relations. Nevertheless, the scope of interaction is broader according to anthropologists who enlarge the vision of interaction to the *action-set* of the actor, i.e. the entirety of an aggregate of people who purposefully interact. The limits of a *network*, as it will be used for the model, are set by the scope and effectiveness of individuals' behavior.[79] There are several dimensions networks are differentiated by. The *density* of a network denotes the ratio of existing ties to all possible ties of a complete set of connections. When we look at the diffusion of less specific information/knowledge, the whole population in which that information diffuses has to be considered a(n) (information) network. This has already been modelled above: the complexity of knowledge, absorptive capacities and the tacitness of knowledge decide over actors' *reachability*[80] within a network. The idea that information and communication technologies would reduce transaction costs reached almost all actors, at least within the industrialized economies. The scope of knowledge diffusion, being necessary for the actual application of such technologies, reaches by far less people, since cognitive capabilities are not evenly distributed. On top of it, entrepreneurial actions are restricted to an even smaller network, since not everybody who understands new knowledge will start a business.

The relative position of an actor within a network, his *centrality*, thereby plays an important role.[81] The *diversity* of the network[82] increases the possibility of innovation, the possibility to detect new combinations. While the sum of connections rises, more opportunities become obvious; with a growing network size diversity increases, whereas its *density* declines: the more acquaintances are made, the less actors will know each other personally. Nevertheless, those *weak ties*, as Granovetter calls them, are crucial for entrepreneurial behavior; a high centrality and connectivity to a diversity of actors, provide access to important resources of all kinds (human as well as financial capital, but also access to charismatic and persuasive co-founders).

A further example for network analysis is given by Aldrich and Zimmer (1996). They use a *population perspective on organizational change* to discuss entrepreneurial behavior. With the population perspective, they circumvent the shortcomings of purely (micro-) personality-based theories. Personal traits, which are unique to entrepreneurs, are hard to support from an empirical point of view,[83] especially when the context of the social group is neglected.[84] Applying the population perspective[85] to look at entrepreneurship, entrepreneurial decisions are associated with a certain population and not with an isolated decision of the actor. Random mutation, *variation*, makes an actor an accidental entrepreneur. The actor initially does not intend to become an entrepreneur but simply slips into it. Thereby, a *selection* process decides over the effectiveness the "logic of internal organizational structuring". Coordinating forces such as market competition are not under the control of the individual.[86] Conclusively, the survival of a certain population depends on the *retention* of its overall technological and managerial competence, the preservation of the fitness criteria. With the latter, i.e. the fourth element of the evolutionary process, Aldrich and Zimmer introduce the idea of networks on a general basis.

The merit of the population approach is that it reduces the emphasis on an otherwise omnipotent economic actor, but it also reduces its focus on individual decision making. Therefore – though following basic ideas of Aldrich and Zimmer – the interest is shifted to the basic functioning of social networks which play a role in entrepreneurial processes.

In terms of firm founding, a social network especially provides access to necessary resources. In the case agents do not have a sufficient set of endowments and, hence, need additional resources, complementary assets and competencies, they use friends and acquaintances, strong and weak ties respectively, to complete their excogitated necessary set of endowments.[87] Not only does the social network provide access to additional and complementary endowment factors, they also have a crucial influence

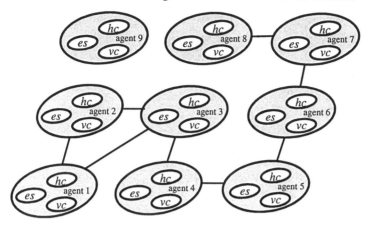

Figure 8.9: The agent within a social network.

on the actual entrepreneurial decision to start a venture itself.[88] Suppose a single agent thinks that he is not able to start a business all by himself. Then, he has to convince others in order to be supported; he has to influence their mental model to achieve a certain behavior, whereas he that might gain even more self-esteem which reinforces his conviction. Otherwise, the lack of legitimacy within the group may prevent entrepreneurial actions and thus, a high degree of innovativeness[89] might be ended by an agent's objecting social network. A synergetic outcome of either strong or weak ties within a network can be an enhanced, and a (by the group) highly valued business idea. In other words, a social network also functions as a catalyst to spark a venture.[90]

Figure 8.9 puts the social network idea into a simple graph showing actors arranged on a lattice. It depicts nine agents. Every agent has a certain amount of entrepreneurial spirit (es), human capital (hc) and venture capital (vc).[91] Agents 1, 2 and 3 know each other personally. Given frequent interaction of those, strong ties are manifest, i.e. the edges persist for a longer duration. When agent 4 is considered an acquaintance of agent 3, we discuss a weak tie, a relation which is less frequent and intensive. Weak ties can stay for a longer time but might be broken up some day.[92] Agent 5 is known by agent 3, at the most, via agent 4. Agent 9 is isolated from all others and cannot be reached by any information for the time being (limits of reachability). Since not all agents know each other personally, the density of the network is relatively low.

All connections, either strong or weak, are subject to change. The way they change thereby depends on the dynamics of social interaction. Therefore, in a further step, this process has to be modelled; even more so, because social interaction is the heart of the evolution of shared mental models inducing certain quasi-coordinated behaviors, which eventually lead to a specific economic structure. For this reason, the social dynamics is reduced to sketch the social network process concerning entrepreneurial behavior.

8.3.2 Modelling Social Network Dynamics

The scope of social network theory is far-reaching, almost infinite. Here, it is not intended to cover all contingencies of social network dynamics as outlaid in the section above, since the aim is to provide a first step to formalize a network forming process of bounded rational agents who possibly end up founding a firm. Furthermore, network analysis shall serve as a tool to gradually step up from the micro to the macro level. Recall that firms are a hyperstructured system[93] which arise out of a social context. Network researchers phrased the term *network entrepreneurs*[94] to emphasize social networks as a hatchery for entrepreneurial behavior. Wasserman and Faust (1994) and Wasserman and Galaskiewicz (1994) deliver a bulk of literature on network analysis which exceeds by far the rather modest approach developed for this purpose.

Using equation 8.2 and inserting the endowment set from above, the actor looks as follows:

$$a_i = \{w_i, \kappa_i, \{es_i, hc_i, vc_i\}\} \tag{8.3}$$

The endowment set of actors consists of: entrepreneurial spirit, es_i, human capital, hc_i, and venture capital vc_i. For simplicity absorptive capacities κ of a fraction s of actors, will be set to $\kappa = 1$, so that the stock of "new" (technological) knowledge of those actors, w_{κ_i}, after the diffusion of knowledge[95] has occurred will also be equal to 1 saying that all those actors have access to the innovation potential. The simple dynamics assumed in the following is that actors of a kind tend to flock together. Again, a lattice is used to illustrate a set of actors. Only the fraction of actors who understand the basics of the new technology start to look out to join a network which might bring up any kind of business opportunity; others are not willing to change their socio-economic environment. Let's say the fraction of actors is $b = 0.6$ that have the personal traits to make a change, initiate new acquaintances and look out for their peers. As an example, suppose that actors have different parameter values in their endowment factors, for example es_i, hc_i and vc_i randomly take the values 1 or 2. Actors with a possible endowment set[96] $a_i = \{1, 1, \{1, 2, 2\}\}$ will change their socio-economic environment unless at least a fraction ϕ of their direct network members have the same values. To keep things simple, actors of the same kind are considered to be all actors, who have an equivalent cross sum of endowment parameter values. The underlying intuition is that not all actors might have the same qualification profile but relatively the same level of overall qualification. An actor moves on according to rule 8.4:

$$a_i \, moves \Leftrightarrow \sum_{\substack{k \in N_i \\ i \neq k}} H(\|\vec{a}_i - \vec{a}_k\|_l)/|N_i| > \phi \qquad (8.4)$$

with

$$H(x) : heavyside \, function = \begin{cases} 1 & if \quad x > \varepsilon \\ 0 & if \quad else, \end{cases}$$

and

$$N = actors \, in \, the \, neighborhood,$$

and the L1-Norm:

$$\|\vec{a}\|_l = \sum_{r=1}^{n} |a_r|,$$

with

$$\vec{a} = \left(\, a_1, a_2, a_3, \dots, a_n \, \right).$$

In order to formalize this process adequately, the magnitude of an actor's direct network is standardized by all in all 9 members. This way, a cellular automaton can be used to illustrated the social networks dynamics with the Moore-neighborhood[97] corresponding to the actor's direct network. Equation 8.4 says that an agent randomly moves *iff* more than a fraction ϕ of the agent i's network N_i differs more than $(\|\vec{a}_i - \vec{a}_k\|_l) > \varepsilon$, with $\varepsilon \geq 0$, in their endowments. Thereby, ε has a twofold interpretation: first, the lower ε, the more the agent is able to evaluate others precisely; second, the lower ε, the higher is the actors' aspiration level concerning his network members endowment level. When doing equilibrium analysis, ε would be 0, meaning that the agent exactly finds his match.[98] Given actors of the same kind, i.e. actors with the equivalent cross sum of endowment parameter values, would flock together. In figure 8.10 the network dynamics with $\varepsilon = 0$ is shown. We observe a convergence which eventually will render clusters of homogenous actors, in terms of endowment sets.[99]

As soon as the complexity of actors increases, the picture looks different. The more endowment levels are differentiated, the more different

Figure 8.10: Social network dynamics with $\varepsilon = 0$.

Note: the light grey color denotes empty sites. The darkness of the remaining sites denotes the level of endowments.

qualification levels will arise. If then each actor is assumed to be looking out for a perfect match of his kind, the search process becomes more sophisticated; more different clusters would exist and therefore a longer period of time is taken to meet a desired group. Nevertheless with $\varepsilon = 0$ all actors would eventually join that group.

Such search, however, to find the perfect match – as it is often observed in real life – appears to be a hopeless venture. A bounded rational agent stops searching much sooner, because either a satisfying solution has been found or a group of people has been mistaken for the right peer. Both, the fact of different qualification levels as well as the respectively satisficing or deficient behavior of actors increases heterogeneity among themselves. The latter is expressed with an increasing ε. In figure 8.11, the group-forming process of bounded rational actors with likewise three endowment factors and three qualification levels but with $\varepsilon = 1$ is shown.

Again, clusters of networks of actors (action-sets) emerge, although these clusters are no longer homogeneous. When ε is increased further, heterogeneity becomes even greater as figure 8.12 with $\varepsilon = 2$ depicts. Compared to figure 8.11 clusters are formed faster, owing to either a lower aspiration level among actors or a more deficient perception, respectively.

To summarize, bounded rational agents, who conceived the idea of a new technology, form heterogeneous networks. In a random process, actors bump into each other and in each time step decide whether to stay in a temporarily chosen network or to move on. The decision constraints are the actors' ability to evaluate the similarities of network members and the individual aspiration level to be content with a once chosen network.

Figure 8.11: Social network dynamics with $\varepsilon = 1$.

Note: the light grey color denotes empty sites. The darkness of the remaining sites denotes the level of endowments.

Figure 8.12: Social network dynamics with $\varepsilon = 2$.

Note: the light grey color denotes empty sites. The darkness of the remaining sites denotes the level in endowments.

The fraction s of actors who engage in such networking efforts, thereby depends on the number of actors who have perceived and mentally processed the knowledge about the new technology. At this point, the role of absorptive capacity and tacitness of knowledge play a decisive role as discussed in section 8.1.1. The diffusion of knowledge is a time-consuming process. While knowledge diffuses, the number of actors taking part in networking gradually increases, provided that the complexity level of knowledge is sufficiently low and the absorptive capacities of actors high enough, i.e. $w = 1$ and $\kappa_i = 1$ respectively. Using the terms of percolation theory: below the percolation threshold (assuming a high complexity of knowledge and a low absorptive capacity of actors), isolated clusters are formed, which can be interpreted as innovation clusters. Owing to their isolation, spillovers are scarce and the *effective electrical conductivity* g_e is low, meaning that the diffusion of knowledge is strongly inhibited; that is to say, it stays tacit within the network. Spillovers occur only if agents decide to switch their network and move on to another one. Above the percolation threshold, the *accessible fraction* $X^A(p)$ of the medium, the fraction of reachable actors during the diffusion process, is high. Networking activities are epidemically spreading among actors.[100]

Finally, it has to be emphasized that the underlying dynamics are initiated exclusively by the assumption of bounded rationality, otherwise convergence and homogeneity would appear and continuous change would die down.

Notes

[1] See Simon (1959).

[2] Compare Hayek (1937) and also Loasby (1999) who discuss the role of knowledge in uncertainty from an applied economic perspective. This literature fits in well here, but the emphasize is to illustrate the psychology of actors in the model derived below.

[3] Compare also Kahneman and Tversky (1979) and Kahneman and Tversky (1986).

[4] See for example Anderson (1947) for details.

[5] Compare Reed (1996, Introduction p. 9).

[6] Anderson (1947, chapter 3) which makes him adjust his behavior, agents learn. See also Hilgard and Bower (1975) for an attempted definition of *learning*.

[7] There are a lot of ramifications in the discipline of psychology which take up the discussion of the nature of the human mind. Pinker (2002) stresses the role of a genetically influenced human psychology, saying that the human mind is not a completely *blank slate* (i.e. not a *tabula rasa* as John Locke called it), which is gradually formed to an individual psychology by perception and interaction. The evolution of human genes cannot be neglected in the research on human psychology. This strand of literature brings Darwinian concepts into the discipline of psychology. Plotkin (1998) provides an *Introduction to Evolutionary*

Psychology which discusses the extent of the genetically driven constraints of the human psychology. At this point, suffice it to point towards the existing literature. A detailed survey of such will not be pursued in favor of the whole system to be established here.

[8]Reed (1996, chap. 2).

[9]Usually, the stock market is addressed when talking about an almost perfectly competitive market where prices would reflect complete information needed to make an optimal decision. Therefore, it would not even be necessary for an agent to collect all the data. But when we take a look at the phenomenon of the *New Economy* which for example pulled the "Neue Markt" in Germany in its wake, serious doubt is cast on this assumption.

[10]Reed (1996) discusses in chapter 3 various models concerning selective attention.

[11]The research on mental models is a confluence of several lines of disciplines: cognitive psychology, linguistics, anthropology, philosophy and also the research on artificial intelligence. The bottom line of mental models is the attempt of researchers to understand how people think the world would work. Thereby, human knowledge representations and mental processing is analyzed. Mental models affiliate also to Piaget's work on learning to be discussed later on. See Gentner and Stevens (1983) for a basic overview. Bara (1993), Green (1993), and also Fornahl (2001) used the concept of mental models in an entrepreneurial context.

[12]Piaget (1974) discusses in his work on "Biologie und Connaisance" the cognition process from a biological perspective. He shows to which extent epistemological issues frequently raise biological questions which go along with the interdependence between individuals and their environment. Darwin and Lamarck serve as examples to illustrate the evolutionary thinking of his concept of cognition.

[13]See also Maturana and Varela (1987).

[14]Note: Here, we see the parallels to Austrian economics.

[15]Compare Brenner (1999) for a comprehensive picture on learning in economics.

[16]Dasgupta and Stiglitz (1980, p. 274).

[17]See Kwasnicki (1996) for a sophisticated taxonomy to categorize knowledge.

[18]See for example Machlup (1962).

[19]See Penrose (1959a, p. 32).

[20]See also Abramovitz (1956).

[21]See Eliasson (1990).

[22]See also Audretsch and Thurik (2000, p. 6).

[23]See Cohen and Levinthal (1989) and, for a concise overview, Pyka (1999, p. 80).

[24]See chapter 9.

[25]Sahimi (1994) discusses the *Application of Percolation Theory* and Stauffer and Aharony (1992) provide an easy introduction. More on this topic can be found in Bunde and Havlin (1991) and Hughes (1993).

[26]Sahimi (1994, Introduction).

[27]Sahimi (1994, p. 5).

[28]The first mathematical formulation of percolation processes was delivered by Broadbent and Hammersley (1957), modelling the spreading of hypothetical fluid particles through random media.

[29]Sahimi (1994, p. 10) shows a lot more of possible networks/lattices.

[30] Assuming an infinite network.

[31] Sahimi (1994, p. 12).

[32] That is, a sufficiently large set of actors would allow to speak of an infinite cluster.

[33] Note: Occupied sites are evenly and uniformly distributed within the lattice. The medium – the set of actors, as it will be called soon – is a static system so that no agglomeration effect can be detected. The dynamics of the medium can be incorporated, showing a possible agglomeration effect via a search process of actors.

[34] See figure 3.2.

[35] For convenience a binomial distribution is used with n=3 and p=0.5, meaning that a higher stage of absorptive capacities is less likely. See program source B.4.

[36] See $X^1(p)$ in figure 8.3.

[37] People's shared mental model on knowing how to ride a bike is robust over time.

[38] At this point, the reader ought to recall the bimodal position of the human mind by Hermann-Pillath (2001).

[39] Myers (1996, p. 2).

[40] See Shrauger (1983), Osberg and Shrauger (1986) and Osberg and Shrauger (1990) for details.

[41] This term is rooted in Bandura (1986).

[42] Compare Myers (1996, ch. 2).

[43] As a reminder, also recall figure 6.1.

[44] Myers (1996, p. 52).

[45] Compare Powell (1989).

[46] Compare Myers (1996, p. 52).

[47] See for example Mullen and Riordan (1988).

[48] Alicke, Klotz, Breitenbecher, Yurak and Vredenburg (1995) give the details.

[49] Compare French (1968).

[50] See Myers (1996, p. 56) for examples.

[51] Krüger and Clement (1994), Marks and Miller (1987) show empirical evidence.

[52] Compare Goethals, Messick and Allison (1991).

[53] As I was frequently reminded that I must not use a *traits*-approach when doing entrepreneurship research, since empirical evidence would reject personal traits as being a crucial determinant to detect "the" entrepreneurs in society, I want to stress that it is not claimed in the model below to be so and, furthermore, in reverse empirical evidence does not tell us either that traits are completely irrelevant to entrepreneurial behavior. Conclusively, I claim to use the traits approach to a reasonable extent.

[54] McClelland (1961, chapters 6 and 7).

[55] As far as reality is perceivable at all in the sense of David Hume.

[56] To recall Hermann-Pillath (2001): The human mind takes a bimodal position, on the one hand, the human mind serves as the (epistemological) core of (re)cognition and as an (ontological) element in the creation of reality, on the other.

[57]False with respect to the assumption that bankruptcy is not an intended successful result of any entrepreneurial behavior.

[58]Communication and social interaction in general are essential for the evolution of shared mental models. See for example Kim (1993).

[59]Though we need to draw the whole picture (from the micro- to the macro-level and the other way round) in order to describe entrepreneurial behavior, symmetry breaking will only be modelled between the two levels mentioned. Symmetry breaking on higher levels will not be considered, since the focus is put on individuals. Moreover, an additional specification e.g. of the firm would not change the basic behavioral pattern of individuals.

[60]Brüderl, Preisendörfer and Ziegler (1996) name more examples such as Brockhaus and Horwitz (1986) and Begley and Boyd (1987), etc.

[61]See Brüderl et al. (1996, p. 34).

[62]Compare e.g. Aldrich and Zimmer (1996) and Carroll and Mosakowski (1987).

[63]Compare Schlutz (1971).

[64]Compare Becker (1993).

[65]Compare for example Szyperski and Nathusius (1977) and Klandt (1984).

[66]Notice that the agent cannot calculate an exact present value of future returns.

[67]Compare Schumpeter (1939a).

[68]Compare Blanchflower and Oswald (1995).

[69]Besides the suggested endowment factors any other desired factor can also be included into the endowment set.

[70]See Blanchflower and Oswald (1995).

[71]Once we divide the actors in different groups, such as potential entrepreneurs without financial capital and venture capitalists, the risk can be shifted among those populations. Hence, the entrepreneurial agent needs not be the risk bearer. This goes along the lines of Schumpeter (1939a, chapter: Entrepreneur).

[72]Each component is the result of a cumulative evolutionary process which will not be discussed in this context. With respect to an empirical application, each component requires sector-specific observations.

[73]Wasserman and Faust (1994, p. 7).

[74]See Penrose (1959b).

[75]Compare Foss (1993)

[76]See Coase (1937),Penrose (1959b), Demsetz (1973) and Wernerfelt (1984). Their work will definitely give enough inspiration to extent the model in this respect.

[77]Compare Granovetter (1973) and Granovetter (1983).

[78]E.g. family members. Compare Merton (1957).

[79]Compare Aldrich and Zimmer (1996, p. 20).

[80]The aspect of *reachability* in networks is analyzed by Travers and Milgram (1969).

[81]See Aldrich and Zimmer (1996).

[82]See Granovetter (1973) and Granovetter (1974).

[83]See Aldrich and Wiedenmayer (1993) as an example.

[84]Compare Hall (1982) and above in this work.

[85]See also Aldrich (1979).

[86]See Aldrich and Zimmer (1996, p. 18).

[87]Compare Birley (1985).

[88]This aspect has already been mentioned above.

[89]According to Stinchcombe (1965) the *liability of newness*.

[90]See Efring and Baden-Fuller (2000).

[91]See section 8.2 to see why those components have been chosen.

[92]Solely from the graph, depicted in figure 8.9, weak ties cannot be differentiated from strong ones. Depending on the focus, relations have to be specified further. For our purpose here, such differentiation can be neglected.

[93]See section 6.2.

[94]See Wasserman and Galaskiewicz (1994, p. xiv).

[95]Recall the example of the internet as a GPT within the Knowledge-based Economy in section 7.1.

[96]Only the endowment triple of an actor is considered.

[97]The Moore neighborhood denotes all eight neighboring sites to an actor on a square lattice. See Gaylord and Nishidate (1996, p. 4).

[98]Notice, whether an agent actually tries to find perfect matches with equivalent endowment values is another question.

[99]In neoclassical theory this search process would only take an infinitesimal period of time. That is a search process would not a time-consuming process. The corresponding program is given in appendix C.1.

[100]See chapter 8.

9 The Model

9.1 The Basic Structure

Now, the elements collected above will be synthesized into the entrepreneurship model. The model is designed in a very general form so that it will eventually allow to investigate different scenarios and, furthermore, to implement relationships and specificities of certain sectors. In a way, the basic design has to be seen as a platform approach allowing several extensions with regard to the theoretic perspective as well as with regard to a closer look at empirical application. Section 7.1 outlays the Knowledge-based Economy as an example to clarify the theoretical procedure.

The *intuition on entrepreneurship* has been collected in the first part of this work. In part II, *meta-theoretical reflections on methodology* rendered an approach to a possible treatment of the subject matter. In this part, the *cognitive psychology* of bounded rational agents has been modelled discussing the contingencies of knowledge diffusion as the fundamental prerequisite for innovative activity. Thereby, percolation theory served as a modelling instrument. Successively, *social psychology* was meant to contribute the theoretical foundation to substantiate the evolutionary process of how shared mental models are accomplished. At the end of chapter 8, *social network* dynamics was sketched to illustrated a simple, quasi-random search process of bounded rational actors forming networks whose members share common objectives.

9.1.1 The Static Perspective

The Actor

To model the evolution of entrepreneurship and the founding of new firms, we go one step further down the micro-level and formalize the individual actor's endowments in resources and cognition capacities. The triple of individual endowments has already been discussed in section 8.2, so that we have:

$$a_{it} = \{ \ w_i, \kappa_i, \{es_{it}, hc_{it}, vc_{it}\} \ \} \tag{9.1}$$

Each actor has got a name i. The stock of knowledge about a newly diffusing GPT, w_i, depends on the actor's absorptive capacity, κ_i. The entrepreneurial spirit, es_{it}, describes an actor's propensity to decide in favor of self-employment, being an independent firm leader, or to be a dependent employee. Human capital, hc_{it}, represents the specific level of technological as well as economic knowledge and skills. Notice that this type of knowledge denotes the fraction of knowledge accumulated through education, job experience, etc. and therefore belongs to the commonly used, consolidated knowledge of an economy's work force. The knowledge about the new GPT,[1] however, has to be considered as the currently diffusing knowledge; i.e. the "understanding of the new invention" providing a large innovation potential. For the sake of simplicity, it is assumed that the complexity of such knowledge is very low ($w = 1$) so that actors' absorptive capacities ($\kappa_i = 1$) suffice to comprehend the basic functioning of the GPT. Henceforth, during the diffusion process more and more actors absorb the new knowledge and the percolation threshold is exceeded[2] opening up a large potential for entrepreneurial activity within an emerging market. Last but not least, a very important endowment factor is addressed, venture capital vc_{it}, conducive to unfold entrepreneurial activity.

The endowment parameter values are uniformly distributed pseudorandom numbers taking a value between [0,1000], higher values indicating higher levels of the specific characteristics and vice versa. Actors represented by vector 9.1 belong to a set of n actors with $a_{it} :=$ actor i at time[3] t and, $i \in \{1,\ldots,n\}$ so that we have:

$$A_t = \{a_{it}\}_{i\in\{1,\ldots,n\}} \tag{9.2}$$

Think of all agents as being arranged on a $m \times m = n$ square lattice, indicating a certain socio-economic structure. As long as the knowledge about the new GPT has not yet diffused all actors remain idle in terms of entrepreneurial activities. In other words, all sites on the lattice are considered empty, since no actor yet engages in a network-forming process in terms of innovating on the new GPT. As soon as knowledge diffuses, actors, who receive the new knowledge, become activated and start doing so.

The Diffusion of Knowledge

The diffusion process is modelled with a cellular automaton using a von-Neumann neighborhood[4] to obtain a logistic diffusion curve as shown in figure 8.7. Owing to the fact that only the lowest level in knowledge complexity is considered, the speed of diffusion is taken into account as follows: a fraction b of actors is initially endowed with the knowledge about a new invention, i.e. the GPT. With $b = 1$, all actors own such knowledge right at the beginning; that is, the speed of diffusion is infinitely high. The lower b is, the more time the diffusion process takes. An alternative interpretation of b would be that the diffusion process has hitherto proceeded to b, without anybody yet coming up with an innovation. Intuitively, a high b reflects an entrepreneurial potential retained for quite some time which eventually might unfold much more rapidly than a slowly diffusing technology, i.e. a small b.

9.1.2 The Dynamic Perspective

Networking-matching Process

A first attempt to model social dynamics was shown in chapter 8.3. The forming of networks is initiated by agents who have received new knowledge, $w_{K_i} = 1$. The number of actors engaging in networking increases during the knowledge diffusion process. To keep the model simple, the network-forming process is reduced as follows: all agents with $w_{K_i} = 1$ take part in networking. There will be no discrimination between different networks (clusters). All agents become members of the same cluster. As in section 8.3.2, agents search for similar kinds of actors, and with a positive ε, actors are not always able to find their precise kind.[5] The search behavior of agents is partially a random process. Actors only become heroic Schumpeterian entrepreneurs, once they happen to observe a window of opportunity which is not exclusively within their own power. This quasi-search process is implemented into the model by randomly permutating all active actors to form groups of k actors. Thereby, activated actors which are not yet involved in a firm are omitted. In each iteration, agents half-deliberately-half-undeliberately reflect over the possibility to found a firm as a k-group.

The Entrepreneurial Decision

Taking into account empirical evidence[6] and using the notion of social networking, the entrepreneurial decision is made in the context of a group. The k actors, randomly brought together,[7] evaluate their chances to found a possibly successful firm. A single agent might not found a firm all by himself but rather within an adequate group of people an actor tends to decide in favor of such venture. Thus, symmetry breaking in decision making is implemented. For this purpose, the specific attributes of actors are considered to be additive so that also a potential firm pf_{qt} can be characterized by the triple of attributes of its k members:

$$pf_{qt} = \begin{pmatrix} \sum_{i=1}^{k} es_{i \in k_{qt}} \\ \sum_{i=1}^{k} hc_{i \in k_{qt}} \\ \sum_{i=1}^{k} vc_{i \in k_{qt}} \end{pmatrix} \tag{9.3}$$

so that the set of potential firms at time t is

$$PF_t = \left\{ pf_{qt} \left(= ce_{qt} \right) \right\}_{q \in \{1,\dots,m\}} \tag{9.4}$$

where $q \in \{1,\dots,m\}$ denotes a specific potential firm and m the number of potential firms, i.e. the number of temporarily formed k-groups q in period t.

The Founding Threshold

Each group of actors has to evaluate if their comprehensive endowment ce_{qt}, which for simplicity is equal to pf_{qt}, is adequate. Yet, the actors' mere perception of their common resources, attitudes and motivation is not the only determinant for founding a firm. The actors involved are also influenced by their environment and the respective mood within the population. For modelling reasons, we introduce the so-called founding or entry threshold[8] Ψ_t. It is a "meso-macroeconomic signal" which depends negatively on the growth rate of sector sales u_t and decreases the threshold. Furthermore, it depends positively on exits ex_t, the number of firms in the market, inc_t, having innovated on the GPT, and time t. After a certain period of time positive returns to sale ru_t will be generated, which eventually again reduces the founding threshold and once more spurs entrepreneurial behavior:

$$\Psi_t = \Psi \left(\underset{(-)}{\frac{du_t}{dt}}, \underset{(+)}{inc_t}, \underset{(+)}{ex_t}, \underset{(-)}{ru_t}, \underset{(+)}{t} \right) \tag{9.5}$$

If the k-group's, that is the potential firm pf_{qt}'s, comprehensive endowment ce_{qt} exceeds the foundation threshold Ψ_t, the k actors decide to found a firm, thus the potential firm pf_{qt} turns into an actual firm f_{jt}, and the formerly potential firm's comprehensive endowment ce_{qt} becomes the actual founded firm's comprehensive endowment ce_{jt}. Actors create economic reality. Equation 9.6 gives the set of newly founded firms F_t^{new} in period t:

$$F_t^{new} = \left\{ pf_{qt} : \sum_{q_j}^{q_k} pf_{qt} > \Psi_t \right\}_{pf_{qt} \in PF_t} \tag{9.6}$$

Hence, the set of all firms that have been founded up to time t is given in 9.7, whereby 9.8 gives a firm's comprehensive endowment.

$$F_t = \{f_{jt}\}_{j \in \{1,\ldots,inc_t\}} \Leftrightarrow \bigcup_0^T F_t^{new} \tag{9.7}$$

$$f_{jt} = ce_{jt} = ce \left(\sum_{i=1}^k es_{it}, \sum_{i=1}^k hc_{it}, \sum_{i=1}^k vc_{it} \right)_{j \in \{1,\ldots,inc_t\}, i \in a_{jt}} \tag{9.8}$$

If the threshold is not exceeded, the option to found a firm, for the time being, is rejected by the actors. Consequently, the actors that do not get engaged in a firm are free to go for further trials in the following period. In the case of a successful foundation of a firm f_{jt} with $j \in \{1,\ldots,inc_t\}$ the k actors involved are no longer available to found another firm. At the same time, this reduces the probability for other actors to find adequate partners. On the other hand, according to equation 9.9, the number of existing firms inc_t is increased by the number of firms F_t^{new} founded within a period, thereby also exerting a positive influence on the sector's aggregate sales which positively feeds back on the founding threshold in the next period.

$$inc_t = inc_{t-1} + |F_t^{new}| \tag{9.9}$$

$inc_t :=$ number of firms in the industry at time t.

9.1.3 The Micro–Macro Reciprocity

Up to this point, the determinants of entrepreneurial behavior have been modelled comprehensively. The founding threshold, thereby, reflects the macro-data of a sector's economic development, which influence the individuals' behavior. In traditional economics those data would be taken as exogenous variables legitimized by a ceteris paribus assumption. The methodological framework developed in this work, however, requires a selection module to be introduced into the model to take account of the reciprocity between the micro- and macro-level. Figure 6.1 (chapter 6) summarized the methodological framework in general. Figure 7.1 (section 7.2) specified the framework to the case of entrepreneurial behavior. Correspondingly, that framework is now going to be completed: a market module is needed – appropriate to generate stylized facts which influence the actors entrepreneurial behavior via the founding threshold. A selection process is used to substantiate competition. The easiest way to take into account the heterogeneity of competitive firms is the implementation of a heterogeneous oligopoly, although other models of competition would be feasible. A change of such a module would only change the results of the model as much as it effects the founding threshold, but it would not change the nature of entrepreneurial behavior in the model. Thus, we obtain a holistic approach while simultaneously focusing on entrepreneurial behavior.

Eventually, we end up with a system which is driven by the endogenous entrepreneurial behavior of individuals.

The Firm

The firm is the total of endowments actors bring into the firm. This is stated in equation 9.8. As emphasized earlier, the subject matter here is not to explicitly model the evolution of firms but to model entrepreneurial behavior. However, the need for a holistic approach asks for a rudimentary treatment of that, since the economic performance of firms also has an influence on actors' behavior.

For simplicity the firm derives from its initial endowment set f_{jt}. Furthermore, once the firm is founded, its structure is manifest meaning that the firm is not able to adjust to any competitive pressure by restructuring the firm.[9] The cost structure of a firm consists of fixed cost K_{jt}^{fix} determined by the venture-capital/human-capital ratio at time t_0 (time of founding), with parameter δ limiting the maximal burning rate of firms,

$$K_{jt}^{fix} = \min\left\{\frac{vc_{f_{jt_0}}}{hc_{f_{jt_0}}} \cdot vc_{f_{jt_0}}; \delta \cdot vc_{f_{jt_0}}\right\} \qquad (9.10)$$

and the variable unit costs, k_{jt}^{var}, determined by

$$k_{jt}^{var} = c_{j0} \cdot (x_{jt}^{cum})^{lr} \qquad (9.11)$$

with

$$c_{j0} = c_0 \cdot \frac{hc^{max} - hc_j}{hc^{max}} \qquad (9.12)$$

Firms learn while accumulating output, x_{jt}^{cum}, and reduce their variable unit cost, by the learning rate lr. The initial variable unit cost, c_{j0}, thereby depends on the initial value, c_0, (equal for all firms) and their standardized relative human capital, hc_j, to the best practice human capital, hc^{max}.

Finally, the total cost curve, K_j^t, of firm j looks as follows:

$$K_j^t = k_{jt}^{var} \cdot x_{jt} + K_j^{fix} \qquad (9.13)$$

With its total cost curve, a firm's competitiveness, i.e. its relative fitness is defined.

The Selection Process

To implement a selection process, we have to introduce the demand side. This is done by using an oligopoly model. Although such type of modelling does not perfectly fit the demands laid out above, it does the trick for the purpose analyzed here. Remember, the methodological approach developed allows for a modular construction of models. The sector's dynamic evolution is decisive for entrepreneurial behavior, but only to the extent facts have an influence on entrepreneurial behavior. Therefore, it is enough to generate some stylized facts of an industry's evolution in order to model a path-dependent process of entrepreneurial behavior in a continuously changing socio-economic environment.[10] Suppose all firms at time t face their individual demand curve, given in equation 9.14:

$$p_{jt} = y_{jt} - \eta x_{jt} + \frac{h_{jt}}{n-1} \sum_{\substack{l \\ l \neq j}} p_{l,t-1}; \qquad j,l \in \{1,\dots,n\}_t; \qquad (9.14)$$

p_{jt} :=product price of firm j at time t;
y_{jt} :=price limit of firm j at time t;
η :=price elasticity of demand;
x_{jt} := output of firm j at time t;
h_{jt} := oligopolistic interdependence of firm j at time t;
n_t :=number of firms at time t.

The price p_{jt} of firm j depends on y_{jt}, which is to be interpreted as the firm's quality standard which increases its price limit. Furthermore, the firm's output decision x_{jt}, the demand elasticity η, the oligopolistic interdependence h_{jt} which considers the past price decisions of all other firms, have an influence on the firm's price.[11] With the total cost function in 9.13, the firm's profit function conclusively looks:

$$\pi_{jt} = (p_{jt} - k_{jt}^{var}) \cdot x_{jt} - K_j^{fix} \tag{9.15}$$

π_{jt} :=profit of firm j at time t;

In standard textbook manner the reaction functions of the myopic optimizing firms would be:

$$p_{jt}^{planned} = \frac{y_{it} + k_{jt}^{var}}{2} + \frac{h_{jt}}{2(n-1)} \sum_{\substack{l \\ l \neq j}} p_{l,t-1}; \; p_{jt}^{planned} \geq 0 \tag{9.16}$$

$$x_{jt}^{planned} = \frac{y_{it} - k_{jt}^{var}}{2\eta} + \frac{h_{jt}}{2\eta(n-1)} \sum_{\substack{l \\ l \neq j}} p_{l,t-1}; \; x_{jt}^{planned} \geq 0 \tag{9.17}$$

Notice that equations 9.16 and 9.17 are considered to be a firm's forecast. They are a firm's routinized behavior. A firm sets its price and plans to sell the corresponding output. The price decision is taken as a constant in each period. Equation 9.17, however, will slightly change since the actual output looks different. It is assumed that the turnover of exiting firms, which drops out in the following period, has a positive effect on the turnovers of the remaining incumbent firms. Hence, an incumbent firm's actual turnover is increased temporarily; this positive output shock is non-permanent and disappears after some time depending on parameter ρ indicating the persistence of such a shock. Moreover, firms which produce a positive output are assumed to be able to grow over time with a positive impact, $\varphi_{(t)}$, of past sales on current sales, whereby this impact is decreasing over time. So that the actual price and output look as follows:

$$p_{jt}^{actual} = p_{jt}^{planned} = \frac{y_{it} + k_{jt}^{var}}{2} + \frac{h_{jt}}{2(n-1)} \sum_{\substack{l \\ l \neq j}} p_{l,t-1} \tag{9.18}$$

$$
x_{jt}^{actual} = \begin{cases} 0 & \text{if } x_{jt}^{planned} = 0 \\ \left(x_{jt}^{planned}\right) \cdot \left(1 + (\rho\Gamma)^g \cdot \frac{\sum x_{exit,t}}{\sum x_{surv,t}}\right) & \\ \qquad \cdot \left((1+\varphi_t) \cdot x_{j,t-1}\right) & \text{if } x_{jt}^{planned} > 0 \end{cases} \tag{9.19}
$$

with $\frac{d\varphi}{dt} < 0$ and $\frac{d^2\varphi}{dt^2} > 0$;

g $\in \{1, \ldots, t\}$;

Γ $:=$ lag operator with $\Gamma x_t = x_{t-1}$;

$x_{surv,t}$ $:=$ total turnover of surviving firms at time t;

$x_{exit,t}$ $:=$ total turnover of exiting firms at time t.

Again, though the selection process strongly reminds of a standard textbook optimization problem, the deterministic modelling procedure of the demand side can be tolerated for our purposes here, i.e. modelling entrepreneurial behavior. Certainly, entrepreneurial actions also include the estimation of demand; the specificities, however, do not have a crucial influence on the agents' behavior. At least the myopic foresight of agents and the routine perspective on their price setting and output production behavior imply a rudimentary bounded rational behavior of firms, too.

Now, as the system is complete, the only thing which is left to do is to present the numeric results obtained by simulation. Before doing that, a short summary will help to recall the basic structure of the model from an intuitive perspective.

9.1.4 Summary

Figure 9.1 summarizes the basic structure of the model. To start with, we distinguish several levels of analysis: the actors level, the firm level and the sector level. The entrepreneurial process takes place primarily on the actors level. A set of actors with heterogeneous endowments is given. Actors form social networks that change over time, expressed by a random matching process.

The actors, grouped together by a networking process, constitute a potential firm. Since they neither have perfect foresight nor complete information about future prospects, their decision will be myopic, based on their common evaluation of the economic situation which is influenced by their subjective perception of measurable economic indicators (shared mental model). The more economic indicators paint a promising picture of a possibly prosperous outcome of entrepreneurial actions, the lower the

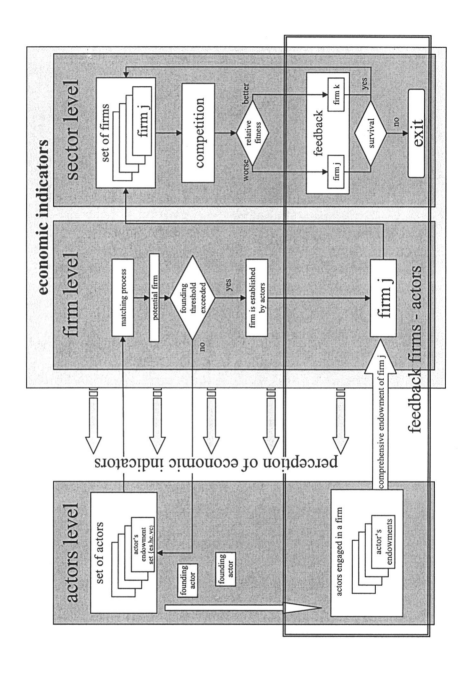

threshold for actors to decide in favor of such action. The same holds vice versa. If actors decide against founding a firm, they return to the set of actors available for another trial to evaluate entrepreneurial actions within a changed socio-economic environment. If they decide to found a firm, the firm is established and actors' resources are bounded within the firm so that they are excluded from a further firm-founding process. On the sector level, the firm is forced to compete with incumbent firms.[12] Their competitiveness is determined by their comprehensive set of endowments constituted by the founding actors individual endowments. The selection process, which is competition, has an effect on each firm either worsening or improving its fitness to stand future competition. Firms may exit in the short run while they compete for the market and spend their money for penetrating the market. Others may not stand long-run market competition, the competition in the market, a selection process which decides over the competitiveness of the actual business idea.

9.2 Results and Discussion

Up to this point the model has been the result of theoretical and methodological reflections and the consideration of some stylized facts in literature. Eventually, the time has come to look at the explanatory power of the model's propositions and implications. Some selected preliminary results delivered by simulation analysis and a couple of empirical findings will be added subsequently to provide a further clarification, albeit no fully fledged empirical analysis, to test derived hypotheses constrained by data which has not yet been comprehensively collected.

9.2.1 Simulation Results

The simulation runs have been exerted for several rates of knowledge diffusion.[13] The set of actors counts 2,500 heterogeneous actors with sufficient absorptive capacities, $\kappa > 1$, to grasp the low level of the diffusing technological knowledge about the new GPT (internet).[14] For the three scenarios, three different diffusion rates have been chosen, instantiated by different fractions s of "knowing actors" who have already absorbed such knowledge right at the very beginning of the scenario.[15] Doing this, for each s we obtain a logistic diffusion curve (figure 9.2).[16]

With a low fraction of actors, who initially have a full understanding of the GPT's potential, we obtain a diffusion curve with a lower slope as depicted in figure 9.2, and so forth.

In order to show that the model also takes account of stylized fact, figure 9.3 diagrams the emerging sectors' total sales for all three scenarios:

agents informed

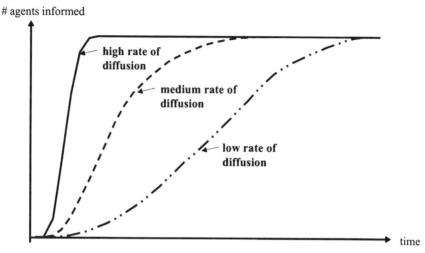

Figure 9.2: The diffusion of knowledge with a low, medium and fast rate
of diffusion.

Note: The fraction b of actors who have already observed the new knowledge at
the beginning of a scenario is $b_s = 0.0001$, in the case of a slow rate of knowledge
diffusion, $b_m = 0.001$ in the case of a medium rate of diffusion and $b_f = 0.01$ in
the case of a fast rate of diffusion.

Once firms are founded, the industry's total sales increases sharply. The
high growth rates at the beginning function as one of the signals for other
actors to enter the market (i.e. to innovate).[17] From a certain point in
time onwards, as competitive pressure increases, with more and more firms
entering the market, and as market diffusion proceeds, growth rates decline
remaining positive though.

Thus, the total sales curve takes a stylized sigmoid shape irrespective
of the different rates of knowledge diffusion. It is just that the evolution
of sector sales is slowed down by the knowledge diffusion process, which
constrains entrepreneurial actions.

Basically, the number of agents being activated increases with the rate of
knowledge diffusion and all along, the potential of entrepreneurial behavior. Figure 9.4 depicts the total number of firms in the market in each time
step. With a rapidly diffusing knowledge, the number of firms in the market skyrockets at an early stage.[18] In comparison, with a slower diffusion
process the growth of the number of firms is rather balanced.[19]

There are first movers,[20] that is, network members who believe that they
meet the necessary endowments at the right point in time and decide to
found a firm. Those early entrants might have a first-mover advantage

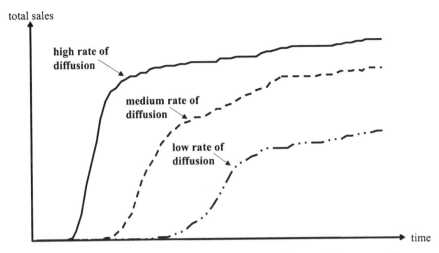

Figure 9.3: The sector's turnover with a low, medium and fast rate of knowledge diffusion.

Note: Fraction of initially informed actors is $b_s = 0.0001$ (slow diffusion), $b_m = 0.001$ (medium diffusion) and $b_f = 0.01$ (fast diffusion).

because they reduce their variable unit cost by accumulating output. Furthermore, there are also late movers who are carried along by a, in general, positively interpreted data about economic opportunities, which is represented by founding threshold in this model, i.e. the shared mental model of economic actors. With a high rate of knowledge diffusion, a reinforcement (or bandwagon) effect makes the number of firms overshoot. Colloquially, we would call this "euphoria". Actors are overconfident and act in accordance with their belief and their shared mental model about the potential profitability of the GPT. As time goes by, this effect is quenched by negative information.

Looking at figure 9.5 we see entries and exits with a low rate of knowledge diffusion compared with a medium and a fast rate of diffusion. Actors get "activated" – receive the knowledge about the basic understanding of the new GPT – and start to positively evaluate the economic opportunities and thus their chances for entrepreneurial activities. In the fast diffusion case, negative information, such as exits, do not occur until the number of firms is already at a high level: firms with an unbalanced set of endowments are doomed to failure[21] and eventually face insolvency. Yet, in the early stage they are still in the market and might be able to purport – at least to a certain extent – to be still a potentially successful firm, since losses at the beginning are usual and therefore tolerated. The shared

# of firms

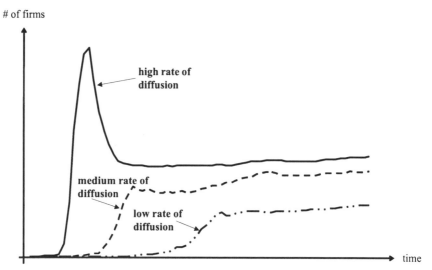

Figure 9.4: The number of firms within the sector with a low, medium and
fast rate of knowledge diffusion.

Note: Fraction of initially informed actors is $b_s = 0.0001$ (slow diffusion),
$b_m = 0.001$ (medium diffusion) and $b_f = 0.01$ (fast diffusion).

mental model (the founding threshold) has not been affected yet. Once
first exits occur and agents start to rethink their attitude (adapt their mental
model), the number of firms in the sector is brought down in two ways:
first, by the number of exits as firms gradually run out of money and second, by an increasing founding threshold as negative information reduces
expected economic profits. In the case of slowly diffusing knowledge, the
same forces work in such an evolutionary process. But the phenomenon of
an overshooting founding behavior is much more moderate or even unde-
tectable as figure 9.4 shows.

With a slowly diffusing knowledge, actors become only gradually informed about the GPT and, counterproductively, negative information such
as exits, market concentration and the wearing out of novel ideas over time,
a less turbulent evolution is observed.

Not surprisingly, the shake-out[22] in the fast diffusion scenario is more
fierce than in the other scenarios. To be specific, in the slow diffusion case
there is no shake-out process observable at all. This is what figure 9.6
illustrates.

In figure 9.7 the founding threshold illustrates the dynamic development
of actors' shared mental model about a common evaluation of a GPT's
overall innovation potential, its economic applicability. With this threshold

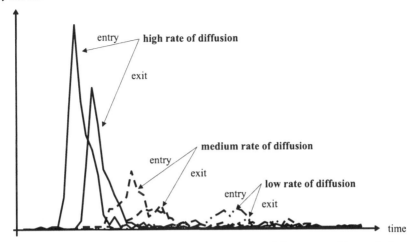

Figure 9.5: Entry and exit with a low, medium and fast rate of knowledge diffusion.

Note: Fraction of initially informed actors is $b_s = 0.0001$ (slow diffusion), $b_m = 0.001$ (medium diffusion) and $b_f = 0.01$ (fast diffusion).

a psychological/sociological aspect has been incorporated into economic modelling, and thus connecting actors' psychology/sociology to economic behavior, and in this context in particular, to entrepreneurial behavior. We see that in the case of fast diffusing new technological knowledge, the amplitude of the founding threshold at the beginning of an industry's evolution is very high. A therefore more fierce shake-out process – as a lot of less competitive firms are founded – entails a rebound effect as indicated by a fast rising founding threshold. Only when the industry's return on sales becomes positive, again, does the founding threshold slowly start to decrease until a gradual obsolescence of technology eventually increases the founding threshold for a last time heralding the end of a technology's economic application.[23]

Up to now, the micro-behavior of agents, their endowment, their social networking process and the symmetry breaking in economic behavior considering their social context has been outlaid. With the founding threshold we manage to make the connection from the macro- to the micro-level, which we need in order to explain entrepreneurial behavior. However, with rationally bounded agents we cannot simply aggregated micro-behavior to the macro-level, as is the case when perfect rationality, optimality and hence deterministic behavior is assumed. Nevertheless, micro behavior is crucial for the macro-level performance, a connection which has not been

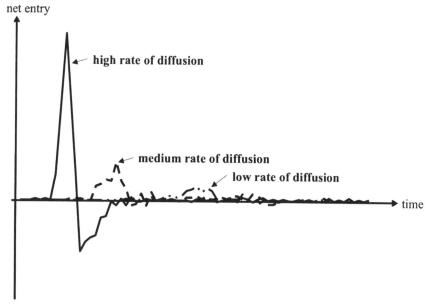

Figure 9.6: Net entry of firms with a low, medium and high rate of knowledge diffusion.

Note: Fraction of initially informed actors is $b_s = 0.0001$ (slow diffusion),
$b_m = 0.001$ (medium diffusion) and $b_f = 0.01$ (fast diffusion).

modelled owing to symmetry breaking which occurs when moving from
the micro- to the macro-level. Regardless of the exact processes of market competition and a sector's evolution, since the demand side has not
been modelled accurately, it suffices to produce stylized facts on the firm
and sector level, which have a decisive influence on entrepreneurial behavior. Indeed, actors are not able to calculate present values of potential
entrepreneurial actions, they have to cope with true uncertainty and evaluate the economic applicability of a technology, i.e. an industry's future
development to justify their actions. They have to act on existing data of
the market. Using the methodological framework in figure 7.1, a modular
construction of the model becomes possible. Once the demand side, that
is market competition, is modelled more precisely, the oligopoly module
can be substituted for a new evolutionary theory of the firm and ceteris
paribus (with respect to the stylized fact considered to be decisive for entrepreneurial behavior) will not change actors' entrepreneurial behavior.

For a last step, the stylized facts produced by the model will be illustrated. As the reader has already understood, industry life cycle theory
tells the story about the stylized facts generated by the model. Note that

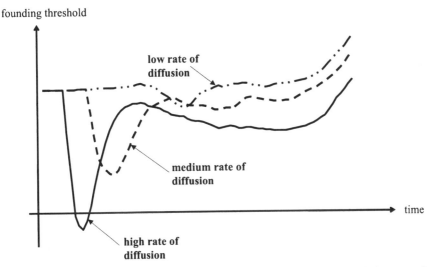

founding threshold

low rate of
diffusion

medium rate of
diffusion

time

high rate of
diffusion

Figure 9.7: The founding threshold with a low, medium and high rate of
        knowledge diffusion.

Note: Fraction of initially informed actors is $b_s = 0.0001$ (slow diffusion),
$b_m = 0.001$ (medium diffusion) and $b_f = 0.01$ (fast diffusion).

the model does not explain the determinants of an industry life cycle in particular, but rather puts entrepreneurial behavior into the context of industry life cycle theory.

Entrepreneurial behavior is the underlying driving force of the endogenous evolution of an industry. Klepper (1997) summarizes some of the literature on industry life cycles as by Williamson (1975), Abernathy and Utterback (1978) and Drew (1987). Although each of these come from a different stance such as the transaction cost, a technological and a management strategy perspective, respectively, the basic dynamics of an industry's life cycle resemble, despite the fact that those concepts differ in the number of phases an industry life cycle may consist of. Klepper (1997, p. 149) argues that the differentiation of stages seems rather arbitrary.[24] Nevertheless, such a distinction of stages, which the model clearly suggests, will be made.

Each of figures 9.8, 9.9 and 9.10 depict the stylized facts of an industry life cycle contingent to different rates of knowledge diffusion. We distinguish five stages an industry life cycle passes through. Considering figure 9.8 starting with stage I: the exploratory, embryonic phase is characterized by a high degree of uncertainty and a high level of innovation. As firm entry rapidly grows and total sales start to increase, the founding threshold plummets. In stage II, the net entry rate reaches its peak and slowly diminishes with a still positively growing output. Hence the number of firms has not reached its maximum yet, while the founding threshold has already passed its trough and gradually increases as more and more exits occur. In the third stage, a shake-out period lowers net entry below zero. The founding threshold is increasing and the total number of firms starts to decrease too. Sales growth rates decline. Stage IV shows a less turbulent development. Net entry is close to zero, so that the number of overall firms stays roughly the same. The total sales growth rate stays low. Since more and more firms reach or pass their break-even point, profits will be generated. Consequently, positive return on sales increase, reducing the founding threshold again and thus motivating new actors to enter the market. The industry's output keeps on growing slowly. In stage V the obsolescence of the applied technology takes effect and increases the founding threshold so that any entrepreneurial action concerning the economic application of the now obsolete technology is smothered.[25]

As figures 9.8, 9.9 and 9.10 show, the rate of knowledge diffusion plays an important role. Though we observe all five stages discussed above in figure 9.8, the stage of shake-outs (negative net entries) is less fierce in figure 9.9. The industry life cycle seems to reduce to only four stages. In the last case with a low rate of knowledge diffusion, it would be acceptable to talk about a three-stage industry life cycle.

To sum up, the oligopoly model used in this entrepreneurship model as a modular element, produces the stylized facts suggested by industry life cycle theory. Thus, the macro–micro feedback effects complete the dynamic process on endogenous entrepreneurial behavior; moreover, the role of the rate of knowledge diffusion shows an interesting difference in the evolution of an industry life cycle.[26]

9.2.2 Further Discussion

To round off this work, an empirical part would be appropriate. So far a methodological discussion has led to build a theoretical model which is adequate to cope with the phenomenon of entrepreneurship in the economy. Some stylized facts were taken account of along the path of modelling, whereby some implications resulted from assembling a wide range of ideas found in literature, to build a consistent whole. The model can definitely be applied to many sectors but it was derived to illustrate especially the entrepreneurial behavior in a Knowledge-based Economy. The internet as a General Purpose Technology (GPT) served as an intuitive scaffolding and some hypotheses addressed require empirical testing. Unfortunately, the adequate data has not yet been collected to do so.

Considering the actors' endowments, a lot of empirical work has already been done in this respect. In the model above, the endowment factors were chosen, motivated by theoretical and empirical findings.

The venture capital component   Holtz-Eakin et al. (1994), for example, tested how the "*(...) exogenous receipt of capital affects the decision to become an entrepreneur (...).*" They found a positive influence. A first major step towards an empirical investigation of the Knowledge-based Economy was made by Klandt and Krafft in 2000 and 2001. They collected data on about 9000 Internet/E-commerce start-ups. Klandt and Krafft (2000b) show that the availability of financial capital is decisive for entrepreneurial success. The majority of new firms is financed by venture capital at an early stage and the fraction increases over time. Nevertheless, the initial surge of start-ups began without venture capital and regrettably, the individual financial endowment, as suggested in the model, has not been investigated yet.

The human capital component   Chandler and Jansen (1992) explored *founder's self-assessed competence and venture performance*. Herron and Robinson (1990) also depicted entrepreneurial skills which would refer to the human capital component of actors. Taking a look at the Klandt/Krafft study[27], founders of internet/E-business firms in Germany have an above-average level of education. More than 75 percent graduated from college. A more detailed empirical analysis to figure out specific skills and competencies would be useful.

The entrepreneurial spirit component   This is a rather difficult one. It is associated with the *traits*-approaches to entrepreneurial behavior such as discussed by Locke (1993), Begley and Boyd (1987), Locke, Wheeler, Schneider et al. (1991). The empirical evidence, however, is mixed. Traits alone do not make an entrepreneur. But on the other hand, this does not mean that traits should be discarded as a possibly causal element of entrepreneurial behavior. In the study of Klandt/Krafft, traits were basically omitted so that no propositions can be made yet with regard to the founders' traits in the Knowledge-based Economy.

Social interaction and networking   Once the data is collected, social interaction can be substantiated. Populations can be built to match the empirically underlying structure of an economy's population. Possible populations might be a venture capital population, a highly educated population with an affinity to new technologies, etc. Then, the psychological and sociological aspects could be taken into consideration so that a social interaction, or networking process can be modelled in more precise terms. Temporarily, the empirical data only allows to maintain that most internet/E-commerce businesses are founded in groups of two to three people.[28] Specifically, empirical investigation is needed on the actors' cognition process, how actors perceive and evaluate a new technology, and, moreover, how this correlates with entrepreneurial behavior contingent to the rate of knowledge diffusion. The quasi-random search process or the networking process, which leads to clusters that hold potential firms, has to be fleshed out with empirical data. Even more difficult: The founding threshold needs a conversion to a measurable magnitude in order to detect feedback effects from the macro- to the micro-level and vice versa, i.e. to take into account micro–macro reciprocity.[29] In other words, to what extent do economic indicators influence the actors' shared mental model about the functioning of innovation processes which causes them to make suboptimal decisions.[30] Most of these tasks have been worked on in various fields, but it has not yet been done extensively when focusing on a single sector. The Knowledge-based Economy by virtue of its topicality and dynamics would be an appropriate focus for such venture.

Despite the amount of empirical work that still has to be done, the existing data on the Knowledge-based Economy gives some stylized facts, which also the model complies with. Figure 9.11 for example shows swarms of innovations in the internet/e-commerce sphere. A surge of internet technology firms was followed by internet services and E-commerce businesses. This goes along with the simulation results in the previous section.

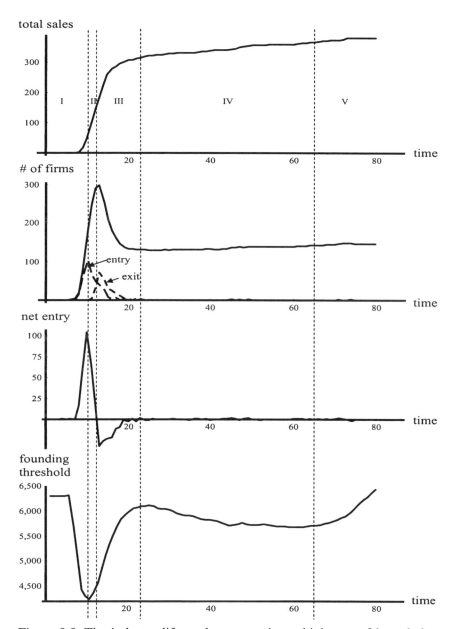

Figure 9.8: The industry life cycle – assuming a high rate of knowledge diffusion.

Note: "# of firms" stands for the total number of firms in the market. The scaling of total sales is in thousand currency units. The starting value of the founding threshold $\Psi_0 = 6,300$.

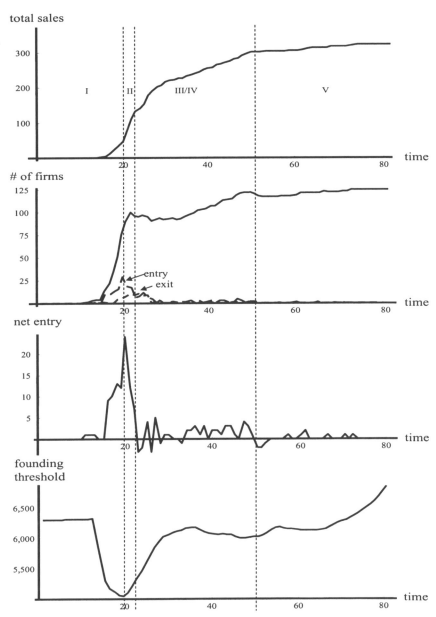

Figure 9.9: The industry life cycle – assuming a medium rate of knowledge diffusion.

Note: "# of firms" stands for the total number of firms in the market. The scaling of total sales is in thousand currency units. The starting value of the founding threshold $\Psi_0 = 6,300$.

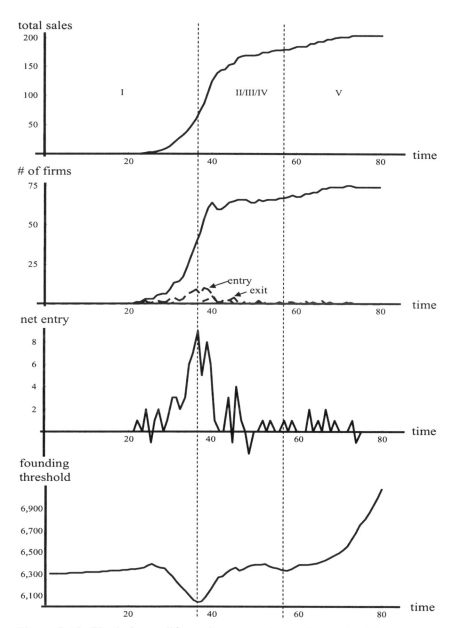

Figure 9.10: The industry life cycle – assuming a slow rate of knowledge diffusion.

Note: "# of firms" stands for the total number of firms in the market. The scaling of total sales is in thousand currency units. The starting value of the founding threshold $\Psi_0 = 6,300$.

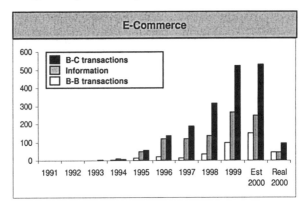

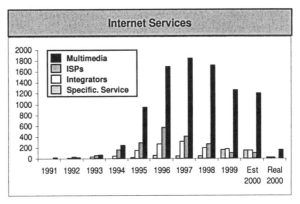

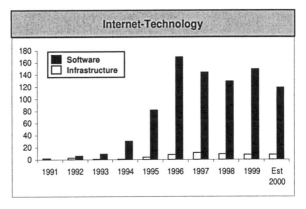

Figure 9.11: Swarms of firm foundations

Note: In all three cases, the vertical axis depicts the number of firms. B-B and B-C stand for Business-to-Business and Business-to-Consumer, respectively.
Source:Compare Klandt and Krafft (2000a, p. 10)
<http://www.e-startup.org/ergebnis.htm> database, Newsfeeds,
RWS-Verlag <http://www.rws-verlag.de/indat/inso.htm>,
Insolnet GmbH <http://www.insolnet.de>, 04/26/2002.

Figure 9.12 delivers another stylized fact: the exit rate is increasing and will presumably be followed by a shake-out process. Although the time series only goes back to the year 2000, a clear rise in the rate of exits emerges. Taking figure 9.12 and figure 9.11 together, a picture similar to the simulation result in figure 9.5 – assuming a high rate of knowledge diffusion – is the outcome. Since there is neither data about the rate of knowledge diffusion, nor about the actors' technology-specific absorptive capacities in order to distinguish those scenarios as given in the simulation study, nor data about a comparable, endogenous evolution of a sector, no empirical propositions to support such counterfactual reflections can be presented.

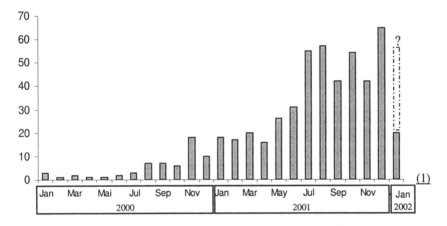

Figure 9.12: Insolvencies of internet/E-commerce firms per month.

Note: (1) The numbers for January are lower than depicted in the diagram because of a lag between acceptance and publication of insolvency proceedings.
Source: Compare Klandt and Krafft (2002)
<http://www.e-startup.org/download/5>, database, Newsfeeds,
RWS-Verlag <http://www.rws-verlag.de/indat/inso.htm>,
Insolnet GmbH <http://www.insolnet.de>), 04/26/2002.

While the last figure only focused on insolvencies, figure 9.13 illustrates an even more drastic picture of "give-ups". It summarizes the total of firms that had to exit the market in a very short period of time. Here, exit is used in its broadest sense: mergers and acquisitions, insolvencies, shutdowns, etc. The exit rate dramatically increased from July 2000 to January 2002. Starting with 676 operating firms in early July 2000, an accelerating selection process reduced incumbent firms by 274 exits. Thereby insolvency is the major cause of exit; a stylized fact which is also represented in the simulation analysis in figure 9.5. Furthermore, venture-capital-financed firms apparently face a higher risk of insolvency than non-venture-capital-financed firms.[31] This supports the idea that an imbalanced set of a firm's endowments leads to failure owing to a lack of adaptability, the incapability to cope with a rapid growth strategy enforced by the availability of a huge amount of financial capital.

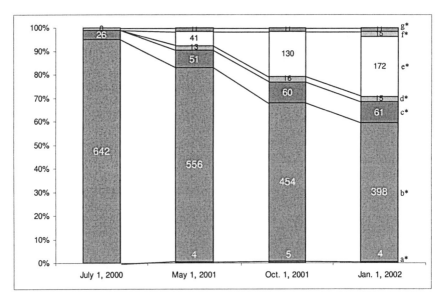

Figure 9.13: Overall exits of internet/E-commerce firms.

Note: a*: firms not trackable, b*: still incumbent firms, c*: firms acquired by others, d*: firms having merged with others, e*: insolvent firms and shutdowns, f*: firms that exit after having merged with others, g*: early-phase give-ups.
Source: Compare Klandt and Krafft (2002)
<http://www.e-startup.org/download/10>, database, Newsfeeds,
RWS-Verlag <http://www.rws-verlag.de/indat/inso.htm>,
Insolnet GmbH <http://www.insolnet.de>, 04/26/2002.

The empirical findings support the theoretical implications of the model. As far as the evidence exists, the empirical phenomena of the Knowledge-based Economy – in particular when considering the internet – suggests that it be classified as a case of *fast knowledge diffusion*: the wave of entries has almost peaked before the wave of exits even started.

There are also other examples which draw similar conclusions to the ones of the model. The appropriate empirical work about industry life cycles we find for example in Klepper (2002).[32] He investigates several industries: the automotive, the tire, the television and the antibiotics industry. He diagrams entries, exits and the overall number of firms in those industries. In contrast to the internet industry, where exits and a shake-out occur with quite a lag, we find that in the automobile and the tire industries entries are more closely followed by exits.

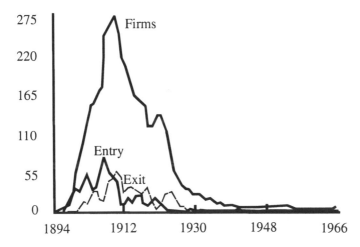

Figure 9.14: Entries and exits in the automobile industry.

The automobile industry (figure 9.14) started in 1895 with a low rate of entry but then rose quickly to peak in 1907 at 82 entries. After 1910 entry was much lower and almost negligible after 1923. The maximum number of firms (271) in 1909 was reduced by 60 percent till 1923. Since the growth rate of output was very high in that period the shake-out cannot be attributed to a decline in the market.[33] This supports the oligopoly idea as it is implemented in the model. The tyre industry draws a similar picture. Concerning the rate of knowledge diffusion, the automobile as well as the tire industry are better classified as examples of slower diffusion compared to the internet case. Nonetheless, this needs further investigation in order to come to a more precise conclusion.

The television industry did not start before the end of World War II. The peak of entry was in 1948, only a few years after the industry's beginning. With 105 incumbent firms, the maximum of firms in this industry was also reached very early in its life cycle in 1949. In 1959 the number of firms came down to only 36 percent of the peak. Compared to the automobile industry, stage I of the industry life cycle lasted only about 3 years (automobile: about 12 years), stage III, the period of extreme shake-outs took only 10 years to bring the number of firms down to a share of 36 percent of its peak compared to about a duration of about 14 years in the automobile industry to render still 40 percent of its peak.

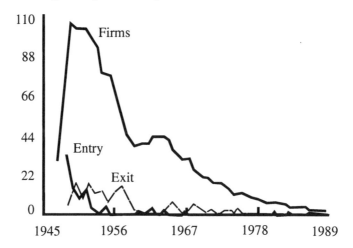

Figure 9.15: Entries and exits in the television industry.

Source: Klepper (2002, p. 44). Copyright © 2002. Reprinted by permission of RAND.

This suggests that the television industry may be ranked after the internet but before the automobile industry, concerning a classification along the lines of the model.

Looking at the penicillin industry, we observe a more balanced development. All firms founded had experience in this sector (pharmaceutical and chemical producers). In World War II the government selected the 20 most qualified firms to engage in the production of penicillin. Therefore, the penicillin industry represents a special case in terms of entrepreneurial behavior. The restrictions on market entry was not abolished before the end of World War II, but the entry of new firms remained modest, peaking in 1952 with 30 firms in total. Also the shake-out was modest and eventually reached its low after about 40 years with a 30 percent fraction of its peak. Hence, the conclusion would be to categorize the penicillin industry a case of slow diffusion according to the model.

Certainly, it has to be recalled at this point that the demand side has not been modelled profoundly, which explains why the curve in the simulation runs do not finally follow the empirical ones that closely. Therefore, the long-term selection process that decides over the long-term number of firms in the industry is rather static and therefore rather arbitrary in the model. Furthermore, it is not meant to explain industry life cycles. The purpose simply is to bring entrepreneurial behavior into the dynamic context of industry life cycle theory, which explains to a large extent the evolution of an industry life cycle.

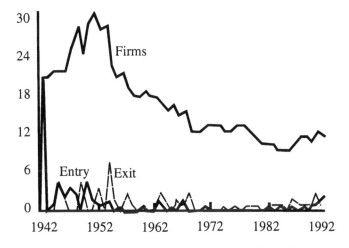

Figure 9.16: Entries and exits in the penicillin industry.

Source: Klepper (2002, p. 44). Copyright © 2002. Reprinted by permission of RAND.

Therefore, it will be necessary to make the connection between the model and economic fields also from an empirical perspective. In order to test the core propositions of the model, the psychological, sociological processes, that is, the fundamental determinants of human decision making in terms of entrepreneurial behavior, additional data has to be collected and brought into the context of economic behavior. It has to be emphasized that this ought to be done by focusing on a certain sector, so that eclecticism is overcome not only from a theoretical perspective – as done in this work – but also from an empirical one.

Notes

[1] For a reminder see section 7.1.

[2] See section 8.1.1.

[3] Time is not implemented as a deterministic function, which would ex ante determine an individual's lifetime path. It expressed the fact that an actor is subject to change, depending on the reciprocity of the individual and his time-dependent socio-economic environment.

[4] See Gaylord and Nishidate (1996, p. 4).

[5] See also section 8.3.2.

[6] Compare Klandt and Krafft (2001).

[7] The random matching process counts for the fact that actors are not able to find a perfect match. This is a simplifying technique to implement the notion the parameter ε suggests.

[8]The founding threshold represents the actors' shared mental model.

[9]This idea is adapted from organization ecology. Compare e.g. Aldrich (1979), Aldrich and Zimmer (1996) and Stinchcombe (1965).

[10]An appropriate formulation of the demand side, which fits the methodological requirements outlaid in this work, still has to be developed. Some of the instruments discussed here, such as percolation theory, cellular automata and so forth, will be helpful to get started with a first basic, theoretical approach. It is possible to model *bandwagon effects* on the consumers' side in a similar way as the swarming behavior of entrepreneurs using e.g. percolation theory and cellular automata. Leibenstein (1950) offers a lot of ideas on that. Rohlfs (1974), for example, discusses network effects on the demand side. The oligopoly model used here is based on myopically optimal behavior, which will do for the purposes pursued here. Nevertheless, in future work the demand side ought to be tackled from a similar perspective since bandwagon effects on the consumer side align entrepreneurial behavior on the supply side.

[11]Compare Meyer et al. (1996) and Pyka (1999) who also used such a heterogeneous oligopoly model.

[12]The firm and sector level simply need to take into account the reciprocity between the micro- and the meso/macro-level. See chapter 6.

[13]The corresponding program code is given in appendix D.

[14]Recalling the intuitive example in section 7.1.

[15]See program code in the appendix D.

[16]For a reminder, the diffusion process has been modelled using a von Neumann automaton.

[17]This is one of the stylized facts also put forward by industry life cycle theory. Compare for example Klepper (1997) and also Williamson (1975).

[18]The analogy to percolation theory, discussed in section 8.1.1, suggests that the percolation threshold is reached long before any type of entrepreneurial action has taken place. Therefore: once first entrepreneurial actions, first firm foundations have been undertaken, the fact of an exceeded percolation threshold allows for a highly dynamic process of additional firm foundations. In other words, the contagion process takes place very quickly so that bandwagon effects of entrepreneurial behavior occur.

[19]Gort and Klepper (1982) also discuss the rate of knowledge diffusion as a determinant of the evolution of an industry in the context of industry life cycle theory.

[20]See Robinson and Fornell (1985) and Urban et al. (1986) for additional literature.

[21]This is an idea borrowed from organization ecology saying that once the firm is founded, its structure becomes manifest and will not change over time. Compare e.g. Aldrich and Zimmer (1996), Aldrich (1979) and Stinchcombe (1965).

[22]Gort and Klepper (1982) define the shake-out phase within an industry's life cycle the period of negative netentries.

[23]Certainly, the underlying assumption is that the technology cannot be improved and step-by-step is substituted by another innovative technology.

[24]The number of phases, which are distinguished, differ among authors. Williamson (1975) recognizes an *early exploratory phase*, an *intermediate development stage* and a *mature stage*. The first represents the introduction of a new product under high uncertainty producing with little specified machines. The second phase comprises a period of refinement in manufacturing techniques and a further specification process of the market. The third denotes the established market of a mature industry (for more details see Williamson (1975, p. 215)). Abernathy and Utterback (1978) call the early phase a *fluid* period in which certain criteria of the new products are not yet well defined, innovation is fast and fundamental, and production techniques are very flexible. The *specific* phase thereby brings

along less innovative changes of the product and the production techniques. Work flows are rationalized. Drew (1987) delivers a business school perspective, where it is taught that an industry passes four stages: an *embryonic*, a *growing*, a *mature* and an *aging* phase. The embryonic phase is identified by low barriers to entry, a rapid growth in the number of firms and uncertainty is dominant. The peak in the number of firms is reached in the second (growing) phase followed by a shake-out. Once an established market becomes predictable and hence uncertainty is reduced the mature phase has been reached. In the aging phase the market declines (compare Drew (1987) for further details). Gort and Klepper (1982) distinguish five stages of an industry life cycle. Stage I starts with the introduction of a new product by one or a couple of producers and ends with a rapid increase in entries. According to Klepper, this phase also depends on the speed of technological knowledge diffusion. Stage II continues with a high rate of entry and ends with a drastic decrease in entry. Stage III is characterized by a low or even zero net entry. Stage IV shows a negative net entry which he calls shake-out. The final stage V represents an *"(...) equilibrium in the number of producers that coincide with the maturity of the product market and continues until some new fundamental disturbance generates a change in market structure."* (Compare Gort and Klepper (1982, p. 639).)

[25]This holds only in the case of the assumption of the static perspective on firms. They are not able to adjust to the competitive pressure and besides learning effects no innovation is allowed for. Here again, the shortcomings of the demand side come into effect.

[26]Compare Gort and Klepper (1982) for additional reflections on the role of knowledge diffusion in the industry life cycle.

[27]See Klandt and Krafft (2000b).

[28]See Klandt and Krafft (2000c). They state that on average 1.9 (firms, not financed by venture capital, Business Angels or strategic investors) and 3.1 (firms, financed by venture capital, Business Angels or strategic investors) respectively, take part in a firm foundation.

[29]Possible instrumental variables to be measured may be: the number of articles about new technological innovations in newspapers and citations of technology-specific keywords by using cliometrics; the emergence of novel magazines/journals on the internet; the turnover of such medium; and the mediated positive or negative information about economic opportunities.

[30]Kahneman and Tversky (1979) and Kahneman and Tversky (1986) would be a reference in this respect.

[31]See Klandt and Krafft (2002).

[32]Klepper (2002, p. 44) collects several data provided by Smith (1968) (automobiles), from the annual editions of the general trade register *Thomas' Register of American Manufacturers (Thomas' (1905–1993))* (Tires), the periodic editions of *Thomas' and Synthetic Organic Chemicals (SOC (1944-1992))*, based by an annual survey of the U.S. Tariff Commission, and the *FTC's* 1939 study of antibiotics.

[33]Compare Klepper (2002, p. 43).

10 Conclusions and Prospects

The aim of this book was to develop a model on entrepreneurial behavior. The synopsis of the literature delivered a multitude of eclectic ideas on entrepreneurship. It turned out that the basic intuition among economists has been persistent throughout the literature. It was just the adequacy of the means used to tackle such a fundamental phenomenon of economic behavior that made a difference.

Early in the history of economic thought, precursors of entrepreneurship theories recognized and emphasized the role of entrepreneurs in economic life. Striving to explain the struggle of human beings with the burden of seemingly scarce resources, they pursued to elaborate the concept of the entrepreneur as a unique economic man who nourishes the economic process and appears to excel compared to others who faced scarcity and uncertainty. With this end in view, economists have always been looking for a proper means to structure economic thinking. What pure verbal concepts could hardly manage, the Newtonian mechanics did; that is, to ensure consistency. And with consistency the ends finally justified the means. But implicitly, the means (Newtonian mechanics) did no longer justify an entrepreneur who would be different to a methodologically reduced economic man: the *Homo economicus*. Henceforth, the entrepreneur became the Achilles heel of orthodox theory, a sacrifice of ends to conventionalized means. Without such a powerful methodological toolbox, however, the theory of the entrepreneur got stuck in eclecticism, since neither a suitable deductive apparatus to assert and formalize a consistent theory was available, nor any inductive procedure rendered significant progress in detecting the deterministic features of an entrepreneur.

So it emerged that the entrepreneurship discussion had become permanently interlocked with a methodological discussion.

The methodological discussion – though not claiming completeness – was prominent in this work. The first step was to circumvent eclecticism by providing a holistic view on entrepreneurial behavior, based on a sound methodological framework. Indeed, the latter is quite demanding, and still needs to be enhanced by future research work. Some modest steps have been made, using graph theory and simulation studies. A consistent whole, a coherent apparatus, a methodology which we may call evolutionary still has to be accomplished.

Concerning the entrepreneurhip model in this work, it was emphasized that the focus was put on entrepreneurial behavior, the birth process of firms and industries; a further discussion of the industry life cycle was touched but not chosen to be the explanandum. The core elements of the model are heterogeneous actors, their cognitive process, which fuels bounded rational behavior and leads to myopic decisions with possibly sub-optimal outcomes. The bimodal ontology of the human mind, making the actor a creative observer, was substantiated by the micro–macro feedback effects (founding threshold) which lead to a certain trajectorial development, since such models of entrepreneurial decisions are irreversible (history matters). A selection mechanism has been attached to the outcome of a fallible decision making process – an imbalanced endowment set leading to firm exit. Simultaneously, a dynamic element is incorporated. The market process as well as the changing attitude of actors, driven by their perception of the economic situation, influence economic behavior and hence, economic reality. At the initiation of the emerging new sector, actors have to deal with true uncertainty dominating the decision-making process; actors have to rely more on their subjective and possibly "false" intuition concerning their entrepreneurial actions, which lead to market turbulence in the early phase of the sectors life cycle. As time goes by, actors are better able to understand the new technology, to assess market opportunities and their chances for successful innovative, entrepreneurial behavior; consequently, uncertainty decreases. More precise predictions and more careful decisions will be made so that stabilizing forces set in. The rate of knowledge diffusion plays a critical role, here.

The emphasis of future research work definitely has to be put on the empirical application of the model as indicated in the short empirical appetizer above. Some specifications will be necessary. Starting at the actors level, the actors' individual set of endowments has to be investigated in order to identify the actual essential components that spur entrepreneurial behavior as well as the creative process of generating a business idea. A possible classification of actors and the formation process of social networks that have an impact on entrepreneurial behavior needs to be made.

The most challenging part will be to analyze the psychological and sociological part of the story, how economic actors build their mental models and how shared mental models lead to certain patterns in behavior; and to investigate the way economic actors perceive an economic situation and a universal mental construct comes into existence leading to a bandwagon effect in entrepreneurial actions showing swarms of innovations and contributing to the evolution of industry life cycles. The methodological approach developed here, will thereby be helpful to enhance various aspects in this direction, since the modular system, characterized by symmetry breaking,
allows us to put together the bits and pieces of the economic system to complete the puzzle of evolutionary economics.

Appendix

A Quantum Theory

The modern quantum theory is a fascinating concept. It has been very successful since its introduction, although it seems to be common that no-body has a complete understanding of it yet. It poses strong contradictions to classical theories in physics. Below, there will be given an intuitive and very simplified version of the quantum theory, in order to give the reader the possibility to trace the author's intuition towards an alternative approach to economic theory.

Mainzer (1996a) and Mainzer (1996b) provide a non-formal outline of what quantum physics is about. For a very easy access to quantum theory the internet[1] provides a website which will be referred to in the following to sketch quantum theory. I will restrict myself not to use too many of the underlying technical terms to be found in any standard textbook on quantum physics.[2]

In figures A.1 – A.4 a so-called Mach-Zehnder Interferometer is given. It is a simple apparatus that makes it possible to show the characteristics of both classical wave theory and quantum theory, and at the same time renders the implications of quantum theory.

The Mach-Zehnder Interferometer consists of four mirrors of which two are semipermeable. Besides, there is a source that emits waves or photons. Two detectors measure incoming waves or photons. In figure A.1 we see the scenario of a light wave as it flows through the apparatus. The first semipermeable mirror reflects only half of the wave. The two halves are each reflected by the top left mirror and the bottom right mirror, respectively. Successively, they meet at the second semipermeable mirror top right and, eventually, the wave is detected at detector 1. Notice that no wave is detected at detector 2.

In figure A.2 we add an obstacle, the black spot between the upper two mirrors. Now, the scenario looks a bit different: Again, the wave parts in

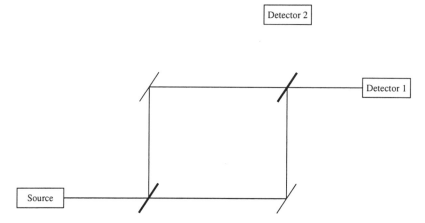

Figure A.1: Wave theory depicted in a Mach-Zehnder Interferometer without obstacle.

the first semipermeable mirror and consequently, is reflected by the following mirrors. The obstacle, however, reflects one half of the wave, whereas the other half proceeds to the last semipermeable mirror. In contrast to the scenario above, we now measure incoming waves at both detectors, detector 1 and detector 2.

Wave theory gives us the explanation: The fact that the vertical wave reaches detector 2 in figure A.2 but does not reach detector 2 in figure A.1 shows the phenomenon of interference. Interference, in very simple words, denotes two waves that cancel each other out because of a phase difference. A wave consists of troughs and ridges. When a trough of a wave coincides with a ridge of another wave (given the same wave with just a difference in its phase), the wave vanishes and can no more be detected. This is what happens in figure A.1.

The same apparatus is used to illustrate the gist of quantum theory. Light waves consist of so-called photons. Photons are very small particles. Nowadays, it is even possible to produce a single photon in a laboratory.

Doing so, the source in our apparatus produces one photon and sends it through the arrangement of mirrors. In figure A.3, we have the same setting as in figure A.1, i.e. no obstacle. Similarly, we detect the incoming photon only at detector 1 and never at detector 2. Hence, the probability $p = 1$. Notice that even though we only had one single photon, something prevented the photon from reaching detector 2; if we think in classical wave theory, we observe interference with a single photon. The question mark in the middle of the figure represents the puzzling explanatory deficit

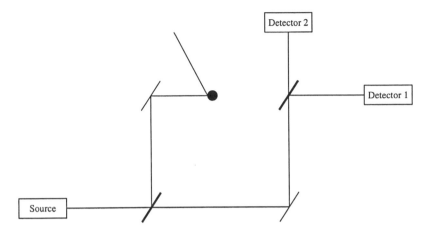

Figure A.2: Wave theory depicted in a Mach-Zehnder Interferometer with obstacle.

in quantum theory. Suppose the photon takes the path from the source via the mirrors bottom right - top right to detector 2, how does the photon "know" that there is no obstacle in order to show interference?

In figure A.4, a Mach-Zehnder Interferometer with obstacle is shown. We emit a photon, and what we observe is again a paradoxical phenomenon. With probability $p = 0.5$ the photon hits the obstacle and gets diverted, with probability $p = 0.25$ the photon is detected either by detector 1 or by detector 2. And again, we cannot say anything about the path of the photon within the apparatus. The photon is a particle but it behaves like a wave. However, nothing can be said about the *locality* of the photon before it is measured in one of the detectors. If we added another detector, we would simply add another obstacle, which would change the setting of the apparatus but not the fact that nothing can be said about locality.

Now, what is the answer to one of the many questions: how can interference occur, when we only have one photon? Quantum theory interprets the wave property of the photon as the probability of photon's locality. The light wave becomes a *probability wave* and the intensity of the light wave denotes the probability distribution of the photon's locality.[3] The photon apparently has two possible ways to take, the "upper" and the "lower" one. The puzzling explanation of quantum theory is that the photon takes a *superposition*, i.e. it takes both ways. This does not solve any problem but it illustrates the paradox of quantum theory.

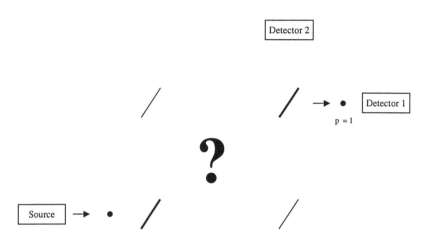

Figure A.3: Quantum theory depicted in a Mach-Zehnder Interferometer without obstacle.

When we repeat the experiment and use a bomb as an obstacle, the paradox of quantum logic become even more obvious. Suppose we have two options: a bomb with a highly sensitive fuze, sensitive to a single photon or a bomb unarmed which would equal the scenario of the no-obstacle case in A.1. In classical physics it is not possible to prove whether the bomb is armed or not without having the armed bomb exploded. In quantum physics, if the bomb is armed (i.e. the bomb is an obstacle as in figure A.4) and the photon is detected in detector 2, we know that the bomb is armed without having it exploded. Definitely, the photon could never have been there because then, the bomb was exploded. The conclusion is that the pure possibility of the photon hitting the fuze (what it obviously did not do) influenced the final position of the photon. This turns classical physics upside down; *locality* and *causality* become equivocal terms and possibilities that never occur influence physical procedures.

Quantum mechanics turns out to be less a new overwhelming insight into a better understanding of time and space and physical reality but rather questions contemporary commonly accepted philosophical, metaphysical and epistemological, concepts. It raises questions of ontology and rejects determinism. It questions a Newtonian world and it humbles scientists in their sophisticated claim towards a world of generally valid causalities. As the Cartesian system reduced nature to its alleged fundamentals, quantum theory reduces natural fundamentals to a pure possibility of indefinite states; it almost seems that nature itself is constrained ontologically, and from a philosophical perspective, epistemology becomes qualified by

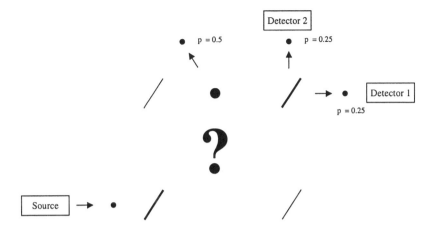

Figure A.4: Quantum theory depicted in a Mach-Zehnder Interferometer with obstacle.

a subjective observer, a part of reality who reciprocally influences reality by observation. Quantum theory leaves a lot of questions open but it supports the necessity of alternative explanations and approaches. Although quantum mechanics is hard to comprehend, if anybody at all has ever understood such phenomena. We are still far from speaking of a quantum theoretic paradigm or whatever, which can be transformed into a methodology of investigation. All the same, it provides us some analogies which are worth considering.

Notes

[1] <http://www.univie.ac.at/future.media/qu/quantentheorie.html> (03/26/2002).

[2] See for example Fink (1968).

[3] Only with a huge number of photons does the probability wave appear to be a light wave.

B Percolation

All the programs illustrated in this section are programmed in *Mathematica*. More than a overview is provided by the author of *Mathematica* himself, Wolfram (1996). The literature by Gaylord and D'Andria (1998), Gaylord and Nishidate (1996) and Gaylord and Wellin (1995) contributed most to the author's modelling procedures.

Program B.1 Parameters

```
n^2 = *lattice - size*
p = *fraction of occupied sites*
```

Program B.2 Actors on a square lattice

```
society = Table[1, {n}, {n}] /.
    1 :> {Floor[1 + p - Random[]]};
    res = Partition[Partition[Flatten[society], n], n];
```

Program B.3 Graphics Output

```
Show[GraphicsArray[
    Map[Show[Graphics[
    RasterArray[# /. {0 -> GrayLevel[0.5], 1 ->
    GrayLevel[0]}]], AspectRatio -> Automatic,
    DisplayFunction -> Identity] &,
    res[[Range[1]]]]]];
```

Program B.4 Knowledge Diffusion – Heterogeneous Actors

```
<< Statistics'DiscreteDistributions'

n^2 = *lattice size*
s = *density of actors informed*
a = *states of knowledge*
k = *name of actor*

society = Table[1, {n}, {n}]  /.
    1 :> {Floor[1 + s - Random[]],
          1 + Random[BinomialDistribution[3, 0.5]]};

VonNeumann[func_, lat_] := MapThread[func, Map[
  RotateRight[lat, #] &,{{0, 0}, {1, 0}, {0, -1},
                         {-1, 0}, {0, 1}}], 2];

spread[{0, ab_}, {k1_, _}, {k2_, _}, {k3_, _},
{k4_, _}]:= {1,ab} /; (k1 + k2 + k3 + k4) >= 1;
spread[{0, ab_}, {_, _}, {_, _}, {_, _}, {_, _}]
:= {0,ab};
spread[{1, ab_}, {k1_, _}, {k2_, _}, {k3_, _},
{k4_, _}]:= {2,ab} /; ((k1 + k2 + k3 + k4) >= 4
&& ab >= 2);
spread[{2, ab_}, {k1_, _}, {k2_, _}, {k3_, _},
{k4_, _}]:= {Min[ab,2 + Floor[(((k1 + k2 + k3
+ k4)/4))]], ab};
spread[{y_, ab_}, {_, _}, {_, _}, {_, _}, {_, _}]
:= {y, ab};

result = NestList[VonNeumann[spread, #] &,
society, 100];
res = Partition[Partition[Flatten[result /.
{k1_, ab_} -> {k1}],n] ,n];

Show[GraphicsArray[
    Partition[
      Map[Show[
          Graphics[
            RasterArray[# /. {0 -> Hue[0.05],
              1 -> Hue[0.2],
              2 -> RGBColor[0, 1, 0], 3 -> Hue[0.25],
              4 -> RGBColor[0, 0, 1]}]],
            AspectRatio -> Automatic,
            DisplayFunction -> Identity]
          &, res[[Range[1, 21, 2]]]], 8]]];
```

C Social Networks

Program C.1 Parameters, Society and Move Rule

```
n^2 = *lattice size*
p = *fraction of actors engaging in networking*
w = *parameter values of an endowment factor*
v = *number of endowment factors*
t = *number of iteration steps*

RND := Random[Integer,{1,4}];

society = Table[Floor[p + Random[]], {n}, {n}] /.
    1 :> {RND, Table[Random[Integer, {1, w}], {v}]};

movestay[0, __] := 0; movestay[{a_, b_}, res__] :=
    {a* Round[1 - Count[Map[Plus @@ Abs[b - #[[2]]] &,
        {res} /. 0 -> {0, 0}], _?(# <= 1 &)]/8.], b};
```

Program C.2 Walk Rules

```
walk[{1, a___}, 0, _, _, _, {4, ___}, _, _, _, _, _, _, _]
    :={RND,a};
walk[{1, a___}, 0, _, _, _, _, _, _, {2,___}, _, _, _, _]
    :={RND,a};
walk[{1, a___}, 0, _, _, _, _, _, _, _, {3, ___}, _, _, _]
    :={RND,a};
walk[{1, a___}, 0, _, _, _, _, _, _, _, _, _, _] := 0;
walk[{2, a___}, _, 0, _, _, {3,___}, _, _, _, _, _, _, _]
    :={RND,a};
walk[{2, a___}, _, 0, _, _, _, {1, ___}, _, _, _, _, _, _]
    :={RND,a};
walk[{2, a___}, _, 0, _, _, _, _, _, _, _, {4, ___}, _,_]
    :={RND,a};
```

Program C.3 Walk Rules

```
walk[{2, a___}, _, 0, _, _, _, _, _, _, _, _, _, _]:= 0;
walk[{3, a___}, _, _, 0, _, _, {4, ___}, _, _, _, _, _, _]
    :={RND,a};
walk[{3, a___}, _, _, 0, _, _, _, {2, ___}, _, _, _,_, _]
    :={RND,a};
walk[{3, a___}, _, _, 0, _, _, _, _, _, _, _,{1, ___}, _]
    :={RND,a};
walk[{3, a___}, _, _, 0, _, _, _, _, _,_, _, _, _] := 0;
walk[{4, a___}, _, _, _, 0, _, _, {1, ___}, _,_, _, _, _]
    :={RND,a};
walk[{4, a___}, _, _, _, 0, _, _, _, {3,___}, _, _, _, _]
    :={RND,a};
walk[{4, a___}, _, _, _, 0, _, _, _, _, _, _, _, {2, ___}]
    :={RND,a};
walk[{4, a___}, _, _, _, 0, _, _, _, _, _, _, _, _]:=0;
walk[{_, a___}, _, _, _, _, _, _, _, _, _, _, _, _]
    :={RND,a};
walk[0, {3, ___}, {4, ___}, _, _, _, _, _, _, _, _, _, _]
    :=0;
walk[0, {3, ___}, _, {1, ___}, _, _, _, _, _, _, _, _, _]
    :=0;
walk[0, {3, ___}, _, _, {2, ___}, _, _, _, _, _, _, _, _]
    :=0;
walk[0, _, {4, ___}, {1, ___}, _, _, _, _, _, _, _, _, _]
    :=0;
walk[0, _, {4, ___}, _, {2, ___}, _, _, _, _, _, _, _, _]
    :=0;
walk[0, _, _, {1, ___}, {2, ___}, _, _, _, _, _, _, _, _]
    :=0;
walk[0, {3, a___}, _, _, _, _, _, _, _, _, _, _, _]
    :={RND,a};
walk[0, _, {4, a___}, _, _, _, _, _, _, _, _, _, _]
    :={RND,a};
walk[0, _, _, {1, a___}, _, _, _, _, _, _, _, _, _]
    :={RND,a};
walk[0, _, _, _, {2, a___}, _, _, _, _, _, _, _, _]
    := RND,a};
walk[0, _, _, _, _, _, _, _, _, _, _, _, _]
    :=0;
```

Program C.4 Moore Neighborhood and Random Search

```
Moore[func_, lat_] :=
   MapThread[func, Map[RotateRight[lat, #] &,
      {{0, 0}, {1, 0}, {0, -1}, {-1, 0}, {0, 1},
         {1, -1}, {-1, -1}, {-1, 1}, {1, 1}}], 2];
GN[func_, lat_] :=
   MapThread[func, Map[RotateRight[lat, #] &,
      {{0, 0}, {1, 0}, {0, -1}, {-1, 0}, {0, 1},
         {1, -1}, {-1, -1}, {-1, 1}, {1, 1}, {2, 0},
         {0, -2}, {-2, 0}, {0, 2}}], 2];
result = NestList[GN[walk, Moore[movestay, #]] &,#
      society, t];
      res = Partition[
      Partition[Flatten[result /. {k1_, {es_, hc_, vc_}}
                              -> {es + hc + vc}],n], n];
```

Program C.5 Graphics Output

```
Show[GraphicsArray[
     Map[Show[Graphics[RasterArray[# /.
                 {0 -> GrayLevel[0.85],
                  3 -> GrayLevel[0.8],
                  4 -> GrayLevel[0.6],
                  5 -> GrayLevel[0.4],
                  6 -> GrayLevel[0.2]}]],
          AspectRatio -> Automatic,
          DisplayFunction -> Identity] &,
       {First[res], Last[res]}]]];
```

D Basic Entrepreneurship Model

Program D.1 Parameters

```
b = (*density of initially informed actors*)
n = (*lattice -size*)
anz = n^2;(*number of actors*)
inf = 1;(*actors' knowledge stock about the GPT*)
g = (*times of immunes*)
v = (*number of an actor's attributes*)
k= (*names of actors*) i = (*iterator*)
foundthresh = 6400;
ai0 =50;
ci0 = 100;
pi0 = 0;
xi0 = 0;
\[Eta] = 1;
\[Rho] = 1;
\[Gamma] = 0.001;
learningrate = -0.05;
```

Program D.2 Society

```
SeedRandom[1]
society = Table[1, {n}, {n}] /.
      1 :> {++k, Floor[1 + b - Random[]],
         Table[Random[Real, {0,1000}, 0], {3}], N};
```

Program D.3 Knowledge Diffusion - Spreading Rules

```
VonNeumann[func_, lat_] := MapThread[func,
    Map[RotateRight[lat, #]&,
        {{0, 0}, {1, 0}, {0, -1}, {-1, 0}, {0, 1}}], 2];
spread[{s1_, 0, s3_, N, sbr_}, {a1_, a2_, a3_, unta_,
        abr_}, {b1_,b2_, b3_, untb_, bbr_}, {c1_, c2_,
        c3_, untc_, cbr_}, {d1_, d2_, d3_, untd_,dbr_}]
    := {s1, 0, s3, N,sbr};
spread[{s1_, inf + g, s3_, N, sbr_}, {a1_, a2_, a3_,
        unta_, abr_}, {b1_, b2_, b3_, untb_, bbr_},
        {c1_, c2_, c3_, untc_, cbr_}, {d1_, d2_, d3_,
        untd_, dbr_}] := {s1, inf + g, s3, N, sbr};
spread[{s1_, 0, s3_, N, sbr_}, {a1_, a2_, a3_, unta_,
        abr_}, {b1_, b2_, b3_, untb_, bbr_}, {c1_, c2_,
        c3_, untc_, cbr_}, {d1_, d2_, d3_, untd_, dbr_}]
    := {s1, 1, s3, N, sbr} /;
        MemberQ[Range[1, inf + g], a2 | b2 | c2 | d2];
spread[{s1_, x_?Positive, s3_, N, sbr_}, {a1_, a2_, a3_,
        unta_, abr_}, {b1_, b2_, b3_, untb_, bbr_},
        {c1_, c2_, c3_, untc_, cbr_}, {d1_, d2_, d3_,
        untd_, dbr_}]:= {s1, x + 1, s3, N, sbr};
spread[{s1_, st_, s3_, U, sbr_}, {a1_, a2_, a3_, unta_,
        abr_}, {b1_, b2_, b3_, untb_, bbr_}, {c1_, c2_,
        c3_, untc_, cbr_}, {d1_, d2_, d3_, untd_, dbr_}]
    := {s1, st, s3, U, sbr};
spread[{s1_, st_, {0, 0, 0}, P, 0}, {a1_, a2_, a3_,
        unta_, abr_}, {b1_, b2_, b3_, untb_, bbr_},
        {c1_, c2_, c3_, untc_, cbr_}, {d1_, d2_, d3_,
        untd_, dbr_}]:= {s1, st, {0, 0, 0}, P, 0};

knowingagents = Count[society, {_, 3, {_, _, _}, _}, 2];
cumknowingagents = AppendTo[cumknowingagents,
                            knowingagents];
```

Program D.4 Networking

```
RandomPermutationList[list_] :=
Part[list,RandomPermutation[Length[list]]]; akteurInd =
Table[i, i,1, anz}]; society = VonNeumann[spread,
society]; r =RandomPermutationList[akteurInd];
permutlist = Flatten[AppendTo[permutlist, r]];

akteurtripel = Partition[Part[Flatten[society, 1], r], 3];
potFirm =
    Cases[akteurtripel, {{a1_, inf + g, {c1_, c2_, c3_},
        N}, {a2_, inf + g, {c4_, c5_, c6_}, N}, {a3_, inf
        + g, {c7_, c8_, c9_}, N}}];
```

Program D.5 Entrepreneurial Decision

```
actorsNewFirms =
    Cases[potFirm, {{a1_, inf + g, {c1_, c2_, c3_}, unt_},
          {a2_, inf + g, {c4_, c5_, c6_}, unt_}, {a3_,
          inf + g, {c7_, c8_, c9_}, unt_}} /;
          Plus[c1, c2, c3, c4, c5, c6, c7, c8, c9]
            > foundthresh];
```

Program D.6 Firms

```
newFirms =
    actorsNewFirms /. {{a1_, _, {c1_, c2_, c3_},
              unt_}, {a2_, _, {c4_, c5_, c6_}, unt_},
          {a3_, _, {c7_, c8_, c9_},    unt_}} ->
          {{a1, a2, a3}, {c1 + c4 + c7, c2 + c5
          + c8, c3 + c6 + c9},
          {ai0, ci0, 0, 0, 0, 0}, {1, 0, 0, 0}};

If[newFirms != {},
    newFirms =
      newFirms /. {{a1_, a2_, a3_}, {ec_, hc_, vc_},
            {ait_, cit_, cij0_, pit_, xit_, sumPj_},
            {kumout_, ums_, gew_, kfix_}} ->
          {{a1, a2, a3}, {ec, hc, vc},
          {ait, cit, ci0*(3000 - hc)/3000, pit, xit,
          sumPj}, {kumout, ums, gew,
          Min[(vc/hc)*vc, 0.3*vc]}}];

firms = Join[firms, newFirms];
#newfirms =
    Count[newFirms, {{_, _, _}, {_, _, _}, {_, _, _, _,
                        _, _}, {_, _, _, _}}];
#newfirms =
    AppendTo[#newfirms, #newfirms];

total#firms =
    Count[firms, {{_, _, _}, {_, _, _?Positive},
    {_, _, _, _, _, _}, {_, _, _, _}}];
kumultotal#firms = AppendTo[kumultotal#firms, total#firms];
```

Program D.7 Oligopoly

```
(*price calculation*)

SummePj =
    Plus @@ Cases[
        firms, {{a1_, a2_, a3_}, {ec_, hc_, vc_}, {Qit_,
        cit_, cij0_, pit_, xit_, sumPj_}, {_, _, _, _}}
        -> pit];
Qmax = Max[Cases[firms, {{__}, {_, hc_, _}, {__}, {_, _,
        _, _}} -> hc]]; pit[ait_, cit_, total#firms_,
        sumPj_] = 0.5*(ait + cit)
        + (0.5*(1/(2*(total#firms)))*sumPj);

(*quantity calculation*)

xit[ait_, cit_, total#firms_, sumPj_] :=
    0.5*(1/\[Eta])*(ait - cit) +
    (0.5*(1/(2*\[Eta]*(total#firms)))*sumPj);

(*relative quality*)

firms = firms /. {{a1_, a2_, a3_}, {ec_, hc_,
            vc_?Positive}, {ait_, cit_, cij0_, pit_,
            xit_, sumPj_}, {kumout_, ums_, gew_, kfix_}}
            :> {{a1, a2, a3}, {ec, hc, vc},
            {ai0*Log[1 + total#firms]^((Qmax - hc)/Qmax)^4,
            cit, cij0, pit, xit, (SummePj - pit)},
            {kumout, ums, gew, kfix}} /; Qmax > 0;
```

Program D.8 Oligopoly

```
(*calculation of "pit" and "xit"*)

If[total#firms > 1,
    firms =
    firms /. {{a1_, a2_, a3_}, {ec_, hc_, vc_?Positive},
            {ait_, cit_, cij0_, pit_, xit_, sumPj_},
            {kumout_, ums_, gew_, kfix_}} -> {{a1, a2, a3},
            {ec, hc, vc}, {ait, cit, cij0,
             pit[ait, cit, total#firms, sumPj],
             xit[ait, cit, total#firms, sumPj]*
            If[i > 3, ((Plus @@ Take[Exp[exitinducedgrrate],
            -3] + Plus @@ Take[Exp[exitinducedgrrate], -2]
              + Last[Exp[exitinducedgrrate]])/6)^2, 1],
            sumPj}, {kumout, ums, gew, kfix}}];

firms = firms /. {{a1_, a2_, a3_}, {ec_, hc_, vc_},
            {ait_, cit_, cij0_, pit_, xit_?Negative, sumPj_},
            {kumout_, ums_, gew_, kfix_}} -> {{a1, a2, a3},
            {ec, hc, vc}, {ait, cit, cij0, pit, 0.001, sumPj},
            {kumout, ums, gew, kfix}};

(*operational performance*)

firms = firms /.
    {{a1_, a2_, a3_}, {ec_, hc_, vc_?Positive},
            {ait_, cit_, cij0_, pit_, xit_, sumPj_},
            {kumout_, ums_, gew_, kfix_}} -> {{a1, a2, a3},
            {ec, hc, vc}, {ait, cit, cij0, pit, xit, sumPj},
            {kumout, (pit*xit), ((pit - cit)*xit) - kfix,
            kfix}};
```

Program D.9 Sector Performance

```
sectorsales =
    Plus @@ Cases[
            firms, {{a1_, a2_, a3_}, {ec_, hc_, vc_?Positive},
            {ait_, cit_, cij0_, pit_, xit_, sumPj_},
            {kumout_, ums_, gew_, kfix_}} -> ums];
If[sectorsalesprevper > 0,
    sectorsalesgrowthrate =
    ((sectorsales/sectorsalesprevper)), 0.001];
cumsectorsalesgrowthr =
 Flatten[AppendTo[cumsectorsalesgrowthr,
                    sectorsalesgrowthrate]];
sectorsalesprevper = sectorsales;
cumsetorsales = AppendTo[cumsetorsales, sectorsales];
```

Program D.10 Feedback on Firms

```
firms = firms /.
        {{a1_, a2_, a3_}, {ec_, hc_, vc_?Positive},
         {ait_, cit_, cij0_, pit_, xit_, sumPj_},
         {kumout_, ums_, gew_, kfix_}}
            -> {{a1, a2, a3}, {ec, hc, vc + gew},
         {ait, cit, cij0, pit, xit, sumPj},
         {kumout + xit, ums, gew, kfix}};
profits =
    firms /. {{a1_, a2_, a3_}, {ec_, hc_, vc_},
             {ait_, cit_, cij0_, pit_, xit_, sumPj_},
             {kumout_, ums_, gew_, kfix_}} -> {gew};
```

Program D.11 Feedback on Actors

```
(*societal change*)

feedback =
    firms /. {{a1_, a2_, a3_}, {ec_, hc_, vc_},
             {ait_, cit_, cij0_, pit_, xit_, sumPj_},
             {kumout_, ums_, gew_, kfix_}}
                -> {{a1, gew/3}, {a2, gew/3}, {a3, gew/3}};
If[total#firms > 1,
    feedback = Flatten[feedback, 1];
    societyflat = Flatten[society, 1];
changingactors =
        Flatten[Table[
        Select[societyflat, #1[[1]] == feedback[[i, 1]] &],
        {i, 1, Length[feedback]}], 1];
changingactors =
    changingactors /. {a_, st_, {ec_, hc_, vc_}, N} -> {a,
            st, {ec, hc, vc}, U};

changedactors =
    Transpose[
    ReplacePart[Transpose[changingactors],
      Transpose[
      {Part[Transpose[Part[Transpose[changingactors], 3]],
       1], Part[Transpose[Part[Transpose[changingactors], 3]],
       2], Part[Transpose[Part[Transpose[changingactors], 3]],
       3] + Part[Transpose[feedback], 2]}], 3]];
    Table[
        societyflat[[changingactors[[i, 1]]]]
        = changedactors[[i]], {i, 1, Length[changedactors]}];
        society = Partition[societyflat, n]];
```

Program D.12 Learning Curve

```
firms = firms /.
          {{a1_, a2_, a3_}, {ec_, hc_, vc_?Positive},
          {ait_, cit_, cij0_, pit_, xit_, sumPj_},
          {kumout_, ums_, gew_, kfix_}}
          -> {{a1, a2, a3}, {ec, hc, vc},
          {ait, cij0*(1 + kumout)^learningrate, cij0,
           pit, xit, sumPj}, {kumout, ums, gew, kfix}};
```

Program D.13 Exit

```
#exits =
   Count[firms, {{a1_, a2_, a3_}, {es_, hc_, vc_?Negative},
               {ait_, cit_, cij0_, pit_, xit_, sumPj_},
               {kumout_, ums_, gew_, kfix_}}];
turnoverexitors =
   Plus @@
     Cases[firms, {{a1_, a2_, a3_},
                {es_, hc_, vc_?Negative},{ait_, cit_, cij0_,
                pit_, xit_, sumPj_}, {kumout_, ums_, gew_,
                kfix_}} -> xit];
cumturnoverexit =
   AppendTo[cumturnoverexit, turnoverexitors];

turnoverinc =
   Plus @@
     Cases[firms, {{a1_, a2_, a3_},
                {es_, hc_, vc_?Positive}, {ait_, cit_, cij0_,
                pit_, xit_, sumPj_}, {kumout_, ums_, gew_,
                kfix_}} -> xit];
cumturnoverinc = AppendTo[cumturnoverinc, turnoverinc];
exitinducedgrrate = cumturnoverexit/(1 + cumturnoverinc);
cumexit = Flatten[AppendTo[cumexit, #exits]];
netentry = #newfirms - #exits; cumnetentry =
Flatten[AppendTo[cumnetentry, netentry]];

firms = firms /.
             {{a1_,a2_, a3_}, {es_, hc_, vc_}, {ait_,
               cit_,cij0_, pit_, xit_, sumPj_}, {kumout_,
               ums_, gew_, kfix_}}:> {{a1, a2, a3},
             {0, 0, 0}, {0, 0, 0, 0, 0, 0},{0, 0, 0, 0}}
             /; vc < 0;

society =
        society /. {a_, st_, {es_, hc_, vc_}, unt_} :>
                   {a, st, {0, 0, 0}, P} /;
                   vc < 0;
```

Program D.14 The Founding Threshold – A Shared Mental Model

```
foundthresh =
  foundthresh - If[i > 2, 40*Log[2, Max[1, Plus @@
    Take[cumsectorsalesgrowthr, -3]/3]], 0] + If[i > 2,
        50*Log[2, 1 + Plus @@ Take[cumexit, -3]/3], 0]
        - 30*If[sectorsalesretab > 0,
        Exp[sectorsalesretab], 0]
        + Exp[0.06*i];
        i = i + 1;

cumfoundthresh = AppendTo[cumfoundthresh, foundthresh];
```

Bibliography

Abernathy, W. J. and Utterback, J. M.: 1978, Patterns of industrial innovation, *Technology Review* (80), 41–47.

Abramovitz, M.: 1956, Resource and output trends in the United States since 1870, *American Economic Review* **46**, 5–23.

Aldrich, H.: 1979, *Organizations and Environments*, Prentice-Hall, Englewood Cliffs, NJ.

Aldrich, H. E. and Wiedenmayer, G.: 1993, From traits to rates: and ecological perspective on organizational foundings, *in* R. H. Brockhaus and J. Katz (eds), *Advances in Entrepreneurship, Firm Emergence, and Growth*, JAI Press, Greenwich, pp. 145–195.

Aldrich, H. E. and Zimmer, C.: 1996, Entrepreneurship through social networks, *in* H. E. Aldrich (ed.), *Population Perspectives on Organizations*, Acta Universitatis Upsaliensis, Uppsala, pp. 13–28.

Alicke, M. D., Klotz, M. L., Breitenbecher, D. L., Yurak, T. J. and Vredenburg, D. S.: 1995, Personal contact, individuation and the better-than-average effect, *Journal of Personality and Social Psychology* (25), 804–825.

Anderson, J. R.: 1947, *Cognitive Psychology and its Implications*, 3rd edn, W. H. Freeman, New York.

Arrow, K.: 1962a, The economic implications of learning by doing, *Review of Economic Studies* (29), 155–173.

Arrow, K.: 1962b, Economic welfare and the allocation of resources for invention, *in* R. R. Nelson (ed.), *The Rate and Direction of Inventive Activity: Economic and Social Factors*, Princeton University Press, Princeton, NJ.

Arrow, K.: 1991, The dynamics of technological change, *Technology and Productiviy: The Challenge for Economic Policy*, OECD, Paris, pp. 473–476.

Arrow, K. and Debreu, G.: 1954, The existence of equilibrium for a competitive economy, *Econometrica* (20), 265–290.

Audretsch, D. B. and Thurik, A. R.: 2000, What's new about the New Economy?, *ERIM Report Series Research in Management* (ERS-2000-45-STR). <http://www.erim.eur.nl>, 04/26/2002.

Baas, N.: 1994, Emergence, hierarchies, and hyperstructure, *in* C. G. Langton (ed.), *Artificial Life III: Santa Fe Institute Studies in the Science of Complexity*, Vol. XVII, Addison-Wesley, Redwood City, CA, pp. 515–537.

Baas, N.: 1997, Self-organization and higher order structures, *in* F. Schweitzer (ed.), *Self-Organization of Complex Structures: From Individual to Collective Dynamics*, Gordon & Breach, Amsterdam, pp. 53–62.

Bandura, A.: 1986, *Social Foundations of Thought and Action: A Social Cognitive Theory*, Prentice-Hall, Englewood Cliffs, NJ.

Bara, B.: 1993, For a developmental theory of mental models, *Behavioral and Brain Sciences* (16), 336.

Barreto, H.: 1989, *The Entrepreneur in Microeconomic Theory*, Routledge, London and New York.

Becker, G. S.: 1993, *Human Capital, A Theoretical and Empirical Analysis with Special Reference to Education*, The University of Chicago Press, Chicago.

Begley, T. M. and Boyd, D. P.: 1987, Psychological characteristics assiociated with performance in entrepreneurial and smaller businesses, *Journal of Business Venturing* (2), 79–93.

Bentham, J.: 1789, An Introduction to the Principles of Morals and Legislation, *in* J. H. Burns (ed.), *The Collected Works of Jeremy Bentham*, Vol. 2, Clarendon Press, London. Reprinted 1996.

Berry, D. C.: 1997, *How Implicit is Implicit Learning?*, Oxford University Press, Oxford.

Bertalanffy, L.: 1962, General systems theory – a critical view, *General Systems* (8), 1–20.

Birley, S.: 1985, The role of networks in the entrepreneurial process, *Journal of Business Venturing* (1), 107–117.

Blanchflower, D. G. and Oswald, A.: 1995, What makes an entrepreneur?, unpublished.

Boulding, K. E.: 1987, The epistemology of complex systems, *European Journal of Operational Research* (30), 110–116.

Brenner, T.: 1999, *Modelling Learning in Economics*, Edward Elgar, Cheltenham, UK.

Bresnahan, T. and Trajtenberg, M.: 1995, General purpose technolgies: Engines of growth?, *Journal of Econometrics* **65**(1), 83–108.

Broadbent, S. R. and Hammersley, J. M.: 1957, Percolation processes, I. crystals and mazes, *Proceedings of the Cambridge Philosohpical Society* (53), 629–641.

Brock, W. and Durlauf, S.: 1999, *Discrete Choice with Social Interactions*, University of Wisconsin at Madison, Madison.

Brockhaus, R. H. and Horwitz, P. S.: 1986, The psychology of the entrepreneur, *in* D. L. Sexton and R. W. Smilor (eds), *The Art and Science of Entrepreneurship*, Ballinger, Cambridge, pp. 25–48.

Brüderl, J., Preisendörfer, P. and Ziegler, R.: 1996, *Der Erfolg neugegründeter Betriebe – eine empirische Studie zu den Chancen und Risiken von Unternehmensgründungen*, Duncker & Humblot, Berlin.

Bunde, A. and Havlin, S.: 1991, *Fractals and Disordered Systems*, Springer, Berlin.

Bürgermeister, B.: 1994, The misperception of Walras, *American Economic Review* **84**(1), 342–352.

Campbell, D. T.: 1987, Evolutionary epistemology, *in* Radnitzky/Bartley (ed.), *Evolutionary Epistemology, Rationality, and the Sociology of Knowledge*, Open Court, La Salle, pp. 47–90.

Cantillon, R.: 1931, *Essai sur la nature du commerce en général*, H. Higgs.

Cantner, U.: 1996, *Heterogenität und Technologische Spillovers: Grundelemente einer ökonomischen Theorie des technischen Fortschritts*, Habilitationsschrift, Wirtschafts- und Sozialwissenschftliche Fakultät der Universität Augsburg, Augsburg.

Cantner, U. and Hanusch, H.: 2001, Heterogeneity and evolutionary dynamics – empirical conception, findings and unresolved issues, *in* J. Foster and J. S. Metcalfe (eds), *Frontiers of Evolutionary Economics: Competition, Self-Organization and Innovation Policy*, Edward Elgar, Cheltenham.

Caplan, A. L.: 1978, *The Sociobiology Debate*, Harper and Row, New York.

Carroll, G. R. and Mosakowski, E.: 1987, The career dynamics of self-employed, *Administrative Science Quarterly* (32), 570–589.

Casson, M.: 1982, *The Entrepreneur: An Economic Theory*, Martin Robertson, Oxford.

Casson, M.: 1990, *Entrepreneurship*, Edward Elgar, Cheltenham.

Chandler, B. N. and Jansen, E.: 1992, The founder's self-assessed competence and venture performance, *Journal of Business Venturing* (7), 223–236.

Clower, R.: 1995, Axiomatics in economics, *Southern Economic Journal* (62), 307–319.

Coase, R.: 1937, The theory of the firm, *Economica* (4), 386–405.

Coase, R. H.: 1988, *The Firm, the Market, and the Law*, University of Chicago Press, Chicago.

Cohen, W. M. and Levinthal, D. A.: 1989, Innovation and Learning: The two Faces of R&D, *Economic Journal* **99**, 569–596.

Cole, A.: 1946, An approach to the study of entrepreneurship: A Tribute to Edwin F. Gay, *Journal of Economic History* **6**, 1–15.

Corning, P. A.: 1996, Evolutionary economics: Metaphor or unifying paradigm?, *Journal of Social and Evolutionary Systems* **18**, 421–435.

Cournot, A. A.: 1927, *Researches into the Mathematical Principles of the Theory of Wealth*, Kelley, New York.

Dasgupta, P. and Stiglitz, J. E.: 1980, Uncertainty, Industrial Strucure, and the Speed of R&D, *Bell Journal of Economics* **11**, 1–28.

Davenport, H. J.: 1914, *Economics of Enterprise*, Macmillan, New York.

De Bresson, C.: 1987, The evolutionary paradigm and the economics of technological change, *Journal of Economic Issues* **21**, 751–762.

Demsetz, H.: 1973, The theory of the firm revisited, *Journal of Law and Economic Organization* (4), 151–162.

Descartes, R.: 1637, *Discourse on the Method and the Meditations*, Penguin Books, London. Reprinted 1968.

Dopfer, K.: 1986a, Causality and consciousness in economics: Concepts of change in orthodox and heterodox economics, *Journal of Economic Issues* **20**, 509–523.

Dopfer, K.: 1986b, The histonomic approach to economics, *Journal of Economic Issues* **20**, 989–1010.

Dopfer, K.: 2001, *Evolutionary Economics – Program and Scope*, Kluwer Academic Publishers, Boston/Dordrecht/London.

Dosi, G.: 1991, Some thoughts on the promises, challenges and dangers of an 'evolutionary perspective' in economics, *Journal of Evolutionary Economics* **1**, 5–7.

Drew, P. G.: 1987, Despite Shakeout, Imaging Industry not Doomed to Being Greek Tragedy, *Diagnostic Imaging* pp. 95–99.

Durlauf, S.: 1997, Statistical Mechanics Approaches to Socioeconomic Behavior, *in* S. D. W. B. Arthur and D. Lane (eds), *The Economy as an Evolving Complex System II*, Addison-Wesley, Redwood City.

Efring, T. and Baden-Fuller, C.: 2000, The locus of entrepreneurship: Firms, networks and markets, unpublished.

Eliasson, G.: 1990, The firm as a competent team, *Journal of Economic Behavior and Organization* **19**, 273–298.

Evans, D. S. and Jovanovic, B.: 1989, An estimated model entrepreneurial choice under liquidity constraints, *Journal of Political Economy* (97), 808–827.

Evans, D. S. and Leighton, L. S.: 1989, Some empirical aspects of entrepreneurship, *American Economic Review* (79), 519–535.

Fink, E.: 1968, *Einführung in die Grundlagen der Quantentheorie*, Akad. Verlags-Gesellschaft, Frankfur am Main.

Fisher, I.: 1925, *Investigations in the Theory of Value and Prices*, Yale University Press, New Haven.

Fornahl, D.: 2001, Entrepreneurial activities in a regional context. Paper presented at the 28th annual EARIE Conference, Dublin.

Forrester, J. W.: 1987, Nonlinearity in high-order models of social systems, *European Journal of Operational Research* (30), 104–109.

Foss, N. J.: 1993, Theories of the firm: Contractual and competence perspectives, *Journal of Evolutionary Economics* (3), 127–144.

Foss, N. J.: 1994, Realism and evolutionary economics, *Journal of Social and Evolutionary Systems* **17**, 19–40.

Foster, J. and Stanley, M.: 2001, *in* J. Foster and S. Metcalfe (eds), *Frontiers of Evolutionary Economics*, Edward Elgar, Cheltenham, pp. 1–16.

French, J. R. P.: 1968, The conceptualization and the measurement of mental health in terms of self-identity theory, *in* S. B. Sells (ed.), *The Definition and Measurement of Mental Health*, Department of Health, Education, and Welfare, Washington, D.C., pp. 201–233. Cited by M. Rosenberg, 1979, *Conceiving the Self*, New York, Basic Books.

Gaylord, R. J. and D'Andria: 1998, *Simulating Society*, Springer Telos, New York.

Gaylord, R. J. and Nishidate, K.: 1996, *Modelling Nature*, Springer Telos, New York.

Gaylord, R. J. and Wellin, P. R.: 1995, *Computer Simulations with Mathematica: Explorations in Complex Systems*, Springer Telos, New York.

Gentner, D. and Stevens, A. L. (eds): 1983, *Mental Models*, Erlbaum, Hillsdale, NJ.

Goebel, P.: 1990, *Erfolgreiche Jungunternehmer*, mvg - Moderne Verlagsgesellschaft, Munich.

Goethals, G. R., Messick, D. M. and Allison, S. T.: 1991, The uniqueness bias: Studies of constructive social comparison, *in* J. Suls and T. A. Wills (eds), *Social Comparison: Contemporary Theory and Research*, Erlbaum, Hillsdale, NJ.

Gort, M. and Klepper, S.: 1982, Time paths in the diffusion of product innnovations, *The Economic Journal* (92), 630–653.

Granovetter, M. S.: 1973, The strength of weak ties, *American Journal of Sociology* (78), 1360–1380.

Granovetter, M. S.: 1974, *Getting a Job: A Study of Contacts and Careers*, Harvard University Press, Cambridge, MA.

Granovetter, M. S.: 1983, The stength of weak ties. A network theory revisited, *in* R. Collins (ed.), *Sociological Theory*, Jossey-Bass, San Francisco, pp. 201–233.

Green, D.: 1996, Towards a mathematics of complexity, *in* R. Stocker et al. (eds), *Complex systems – from local interactions to global behaviour*, IOS Press, Amsterdam, pp. 97–105.

Green, D. W.: 1993, Mental models: Rationality, representation and process, *Behavioral and Brain Sciences* (16), 352–353.

Groenenwegen, P.: 1971, A reinterpretation of Turgot's theory of captial and interest, *Economic Journal* (81), 327–328, 339–340.

Hall, R.: 1982, *Organizations: Structure and Process*, 3 edn, Prentice-Hall, Englewood Cliffs, NJ.

Hanusch, H.: 1988, Introduction, *in* H. Hanusch (ed.), *Evolutionary Economics: Application of Schumpeter's Ideas*, Cambridge University Press, Cambridge, pp. 1–8.

Harrod, R.: 1930, Notes on supply, *Economic Journal* (40), 234.

Hawking, S.: 1988, *A Brief History of Time: From the Big Bang to Black Holes*, Bantam Books, New York.

Hayek, F. A.: 1937, Economics and knowledge, *in* M. Casson (ed.), *Entrepreneurship*, Edward Elgar, England. Reprinted 1990.

Hébert, R. F. and Link, A. N.: 1982, *The Entrepreneur: Mainstream Views and Radical Critiques*, 2nd edn, Praeger, New York.

Hegel, G. W. F.: 1996, *The Philosophical System*, Twayne Publishers, Boston, MA.

Heisenberg, W.: 2000, *Physik und Philosophie*, 5th edn, S. Hirzel, Stuttgart.

Helpman, E.: 1998, *General Purpose Technologies and Economic Growth*, MIT Press, Cambridge, MA.

Hermann, F.: 1832, *Staatswirtschaftliche Untersuchungen über Vermögen: Wirtschaft, Produktivität der Arbeiten, Kapital, Preis, Gewinn, Einkommen und Verbrauch*, A. Weber, Munich.

Hermann-Pillath, C.: 2001, On the ontological foundations of evolutionary economics, *in* K. Dopfer (ed.), *Evolutionary Economics – Program and Scope*, Kluwer Academic Publishers, Boston/Dordrecht/London, pp. 89–139.

Herron, L. A. and Robinson, R. B.: 1990, Entrepreneurial skills: An empirical study of the missing link connecting the entrepreneur with venture performance, Paper presented at the National Academy of Management Meeting, San Francisco.

Hilgard, E. and Bower, G.: 1975, *Theories of Learning*, 4th edn, Prentice-Hall, Englewood Cliffs.

Hirschleifer, J.: 1982, Evolutionary models in economics and law, *Research in Law and Economics* **4**, 1–60.

Hodgson, G. M.: 1995a, *Economics and Biology*, Edward Elgar, England.

Hodgson, G. M.: 1995b, Introduction, *in* G. M. Hodgson (ed.), *Economics and Biology*, Vol. 50 of *International Library of Critical Writings in Economics*, Edward Elgar, Cheltenham, pp. xiii–xxv.

Hodgson, G. M.: 1998, Evolutionary economics, *in* J. B. Davis, D. W. Hands and U. Mäki (eds), *Handbook of Economic Methodology*, Edward Elgar, Cheltenham, pp. 160–167.

Hodgson, G. M.: 2000, What is the essence of institutional economics?, *Journal of Economic Issues* **34**(2), 317–330.

Hodgson, G. M.: 2002, Darwinism in economics: from analogy to ontology, *Journal of Evolutionary Economics* **12**, 259–281.

Holtz-Eakin et al.: 1994, Entrepreneurial decisions and liquidity constraints, *RAND Journal of Economics* **25**(2), 334–347.

Hufeland, G.: 1815, *Neue Grundlegung der Staatswirtschaftskunst*, B. P. Bauer, Vienna.

Hughes, B. D.: 1993, *Random Environments and Random Walks*, Oxford University Press, Oxford.

Hume, D.: 1748, *An Enquiry Concerning Human Understanding*, 2nd edn, Hackett Publishing, Indianapolis. Reprinted 1993.

Hunsdiek, D. and May-Strobl, E.: 1986, *Entwicklungslinien und Entwicklungsrisiken neugegründeter Unternehmen*, Poeschel, Stuttgart.

Jevons, W. S.: 1871, *The Theory of Political Economy*, Macmillan, London.

Jolink, A.: 1996, *The Evolutionist Economics of Léon Walras*, Routledge, London and New York.

Jovanovic, B. and MacDonald, G. M.: 1994, The life cycle of a competitive industry, *Journal of Political Economy* **102**(2), 322–347.

Justman, M.: 1996, Swarming mechanics, *Journal of Innovation and New Technology* **4**, 235–244.

Kahneman, D. and Tversky, A.: 1979, Prospect theory, *Econometrica* **47**, 263–291.

Kahneman, D. and Tversky, A.: 1986, Rational choices and the framing of decisions, *in* R. M. Hogarth and M. W. Reder (eds), *Rational Choice: The Contrast between Economics and Psychology*, Chicago University Press, Chicago.

Kant, I.: 1884, The Critique of Pure Reason, trans. Norman Kemp Smith, St. Martin's Press, New York. Reprinted 1998.

Kastrop, C.: 1993, *Rationale Ökonomik?*, Duncker & Humblot, Berlin.

Kauffman, S.: 1993, *The Origins of Order: Self-Organization and Selection in Evolution*, Oxford University Press, Oxford.

Keita, L. D.: 1992, *Science, Rationality, and Neoclassical Economics*, Associated University Press, Delaware, London and Toronto.

Kihlstrom, R. E. and Laffont, J. J.: 1979, A general equilibrium entrepreneurial theory of firm formation based on risk aversion, *Journal of Political Economy* (87), 719–748.

Kim, D. H.: 1993, The link between individual and organizational learning, *Sloan Management Review* (Fall), 37–50.

Kirman, A.: 1983, Communication in markets, *Economics Letters* (12), 101–108.

Kirman, A.: 1987, Graph theory, *in* J. Eatwell, M. Milgate and P. Newman (eds), *The New Pargrave: A Dictionary of Economics*, Macmillan, London, pp. 558–559.

Kirzner, I. M.: 1973, *Competition and Entrepreneurship*, University of Chicago Press, Chicago.

Kirzner, I. M.: 1990, 'Commentary' on Stephan Broehm, *in* K. Hennings and W. Samuels (eds), *Neoclassical Economic Theory*, Kluwer, Boston/Dordrecht/London, pp. 1870–1930.

Kirzner, I. M.: 1999, Creativity and/or alertness: A reconsideration of the schumpeterian entrepreneur, *Review of Austrian Economics*, Vol. 11, Kluwer Academic Publishers, Amsterdam, pp. 5–17.

Klandt, H.: 1984, *Aktivität und Erfolg des Unternehmensgründers: Eine empirische Analyse unter Einbeziehung des mikrosozialen Umfeldes*, Bergisch Gladbach.

Klandt, H. and Krafft, L.: 2000a, Bestandsaufnahme und Perspektiven der Internet-/E-Commerce Gründerlandschaft in Deutschland, Diskussionspapier. Stiftungslehrstuhl für Gründungsmanagement und Entrepreneurship, European Business School, Oestrich-Winkel.

Klandt, H. and Krafft, L.: 2000b, Die Bedeutung von Venture Capital für die Entwicklung von Internet-/E-Commerce-Gründungen in Deutschland, Diskussionspapier. Stiftungslehrstuhl für Gründungsmanagement und Entrepreneurship, European Business School, Oestrich-Winkel.

Klandt, H. and Krafft, L.: 2000c, Internet/E-Commerce Gründungen in Deutschland, Segment-Analyse: Verkaufsorientierte B2C-Anbieter (Business-to-Consumer, Diskussionspapier. Stiftungslehrstuhl für Gründungsmanagement und Entrepreneurship, European Business School, Oestrich-Winkel.

Klandt, H. and Krafft, L.: 2001, Aktuelle Beschäftignung und Mitarbeiterbedarf bei Internet-/E-Commerce-Gründungen in Deutschland, Diskussionspapier. Stiftungslehrstuhl für Gründungsmanagement und Entrepreneurship, European Business School, Oestrich-Winkel.

Klandt, H. and Krafft, L.: 2002, Aktuelle Ausfall-Raten bei Internet-/E-Commerce Gründungen in Deutschland (3. review), http://www.e-startup.org/download, 04/26/2002. Stiftungslehrstuhl für Gründungsmanagement und Entrepreneurship, European Business School, Oestrich-Winkel.

Klepper, S.: 1997, Industry life cycles, *Industrial and Corporate Change* **6**, 145–181.

Klepper, S.: 2002, Firm survival and the evolution of oligopoly, *RAND Journal of Economics* **33**(1), 37–61.

Klepper, S. and Graddy, E.: 1990, The evolution of new industries and the determinants of market structure, *RAND Journal of Economics* **21**(1), 27–44.

Knight, F. H.: 1921, *Risk, Uncertainty and Profit*, Houghton Mifflin, New York.

Koestler, A.: 1969, Beyond atomism and holism, *in* A. Koestler and J. Smythies (eds), *Beyond Reductionism: New Perspectives in the Life Sciences*, Hutchinson, London, pp. 192–216.

Kolb, G.: 1991, *Grundlagen der Volkswirtschaftslehre*, Franz Vahlen Verlag, Munich.

Krüger, J. and Clement, R. W.: 1994, The truly false consensus effect: An ineradicable and egocentric bias in social perception, *Journal of Personality and Social Psychology* (67), 596–610.

Kwasnicki, W.: 1996, *Knowledge, Innovation and Economy*, Vol. 29, Edward Elgar, Cheltenham.

Leibenstein, H.: 1950, Badwagon, snob, and veblen effects in the theory of consumers demand, *in* W. Breit and H. M. Hochmann (eds), *Readings in Microeconomics*, 2nd edn, Holt, Rinehart and Winston, New York, pp. 115–116.

Levin, R. C. and Reiss, P. C.: 1984, Tests of a Schumpeterian Model of R&D and Market Structure, *in* Z. Grilliches (ed.), *R&D, Patents and Productivity*, University of Chicago Press, Chicago.

Levinthal, D. A.: 1991, Random walks and organizational mortality, *Administrative Science Quarterly* (36), 397–420.

Loasby, B. J.: 1976, *Choice, Complexity and Ignorance*, Cambridge University Press, Cambridge.

Loasby, B. J.: 1999, *Knowledge, Institutions and Evolution in Economics*, Routledge, New York.

Locke, E. A.: 1993, The traits of american business heroes, Working Paper, University of Maryland.

Locke, E. A., Wheeler, J. K., Schneider, J. et al.: 1991, *The Essence of Leadership*, Lexington Books, New York.

Locke, J.: 1690, An essay concerning human understanding, New York: Dover. Reprinted 1959.

Lundvall, B.-A.: 1998, The learning economy: Challenges to economic theory and policy, *in* B. J. K. Nielsen (ed.), *Institutions and Economic Change: New Perspectives on Markets, Firms and Technology*, Edward Elgar, Cheltenham.

Lundvall, B. and Johnson, B.: 1994, The learning economy, *Journal of Industry Studies* **1**(2), 23–42.

Machlup, F.: 1962, *The Production and Distribution of Knowledge in the United States*, Princeton University Press, Princeton, NJ.

Mainzer, K.: 1996a, *Materie*, Beck, Munich.

Mainzer, K.: 1996b, *Thinking in complexity*, 2nd edn, Springer Verlag, Berlin.

Mäki, U.: 1989, Realism in economics, *Ricerche Economiche* **43**, 176–198.

Mäki, U.: 1998, Realism, *in* J. B. Davis, D. W. Hands and U. Mäki (eds), *Handbook of Economic Methodology*, Edward Elgar, Cheltenham, pp. 409–413.

Marks, G. and Miller, N.: 1987, Ten years of research on the false-consensus effect. an empirical and theoretical review, *Psychological Bulletin* (102), 72–90.

Marshall, A.: 1948, *Principles of Economics*, 8th edn, MacMillan and Co., London. First published 1920.

Maturana, H. R. and Varela, F. J.: 1987, *Der Baum der Erkenntnis*, Scherz, Bern and Munich.

McClelland, D. C.: 1961, *The Achieving Society*, Van Nostrand Reinhold, New York.

Menger, C.: 1968, *Grundsätze der Volkswirtschaftslehre. Gesammelte Werke*, Vol. 1, Tübingen.

Merton, R. K.: 1957, The role-set problems in sociological theory, *British Journal of Sociology* (8), 106–120.

Metcalfe, J. S.: 1994a, Competition, fisher's principle and increasing returns to selection, *Journal of Evolutionary Economics* **4**, 327–346.

Metcalfe, J. S.: 1994b, Evolution, economics, and technology policy, *Economic Journal* **104**, 931–944.

Metcalfe, J. S., Fonseca, M. D. and Ramlogan, R.: 2000, Innovation, growth and competition: Evolving complexity or complex evolution. Paper prepared for the Complexity and Complex Systems in Industry Conference 19th – 20th September, University of Warwick.

Meyer, B. et al.: 1996, Schumpeterian competition in heterogeneous oligopolies, *Journal of Evolutionary Economics* **6**, 411–423.

Mill, J. S.: 1848, *Principles of Political Economy*, Longmans, London. Reprinted 1909.

Mill, J. S.: 1962, *On Bentham and Coleridge*, Harper Torchbook, New York.

Mullen, B. and Riordan, C. A.: 1988, Self-serving attributions for performance in naturalistic settings: A metaanalytic review, *Journal of Applied Social Psychology* (18), 3–22.

Myers, D. G.: 1996, *Social psychology*, 5th edn, McGraw-Hill, New York.

Nelson, R. R.: 1995, Recent evolutionary theorizing about economic change, *Journal of Economic Literature* **XXXIII**, 48–90.

Nelson, R. R. and Winter, S. G.: 1982, *An Evolutionary Theory of Economic Change*, Cambridge University Press, Cambridge.

Neumann, K. and Morlock, M.: 1993, *Operations Resarch*, Carl Hanser Verlag, Munich.

O'Driscoll, G. and Rizzo, M.: 1986, Subjectivism, uncertainty and rules, *in* I. Kirzner (ed.), *Subjectivism, Intelligibility and Economic Understanding*, Macmillan, London, pp. 252–267.

Osberg, T. M. and Shrauger, J. S.: 1986, Self-prediction: Exploring the parameters of accuracy, *Journal of Personality and Social Psychology* (51), 1044–1057.

Osberg, T. M. and Shrauger, J. S.: 1990, The role of self-prediction in psychological assessment, *in* J. N. Butcher and C. D. Spielberger (eds), *Advances in Personality Assessment*, Vol. 8, Erlbaum, Hillsdale, NJ.

Penrose, E.: 1959a, *The Theory of the Growth of the Firm*, Basil Blackwell, Oxford.

Penrose, E. T.: 1959b, *The Theory of the Growth of the Firm*, Oxford University Press, Oxford.

Penrose, R.: 1990, *The Emperor's New Mind*, Oxford University Press, Oxford.

Perlman, M. and McCann, C. R.: 1998, *The Pillars of Economic Understanding*, The University of Michigan Press, Ann Arbor.

Pesciarelli, E.: 1986, *Smith, Bentham, and the Development of Contrasting Ideas on Entrepreneurship*, 21, History of Political Economy.

Piaget, J.: 1974, *Biologie und Erkenntnis*, Conditio Humana, Fischer, Frankfurt am Main.

Pinker, S.: 2002, *The Blank Slate: The Modern Denial of Human Nature*, Viking Penguin Putnam, New York.

Plotkin, H. C.: 1998, *Evolution in Mind: An Introduction to Evolutionary Psychology*, Harvard University Press, Harvard, MA.

Polanyi, M.: 1958, *Personal Knowledge: Towards a Post-Critical Philosophy*, Routledge and Kegan Paul, London.

Popper, K.: 1959, *The Logic of Scientific Discovery*, Basic Books, New York.

Porter, M.: 1980, *Competitive Strategy*, Free Press, New York.

Potts, J.: 2000, *The New Evolutionary Mircoreconomics*, Edward Elgar, Cheltenham.

Powell, J.: 1989, *Happiness Is an Inside Job*, Tabor, Valencia, CA.

Prigogine, I.: 1987, Exploring complexity, *European Journal of Operational Research* (30), 97–103.

Pyka, A.: 1999, *Der kollektive Innovationsprozeß. Eine theoretische Analyse informeller Netzwerke und absorptiver Fähigkeiten*, Duncker & Humblot, Berlin.

Redlich, F.: 1949, *The Origin of the Concepts of "Entrepreneur" and "Creative Entrepreneur"*, Explorations in Entrepreneurial History.

Reed, K. S.: 1996, *Cognition*, 4th edn, Brooks/Cole Publishing, Pacific Grove, CA.

Ricardo, D.: 1821, *On the Principles of Political Economy and Taxation*, 3rd edn, John Murray, London.

Riedel, A. F. J.: 1838–43, *Nationalökonomie oder Volkswirtschaft Dargestellt*, Vol. 3, F. H. Morin, Berlin.

Robinson, J.: 1969, *The economics of imperfect competition*, 2nd edn, MacMillan, London.

Robinson, W. T. and Fornell, C.: 1985, Sources of market pioneer advantages in consumer goods industries, *Journal of Marketing Research* **XXII**, 305–317.

Rohlfs, J.: 1974, A theory of interdependent demand for a communications service, *Bell Journal of Economics and Management Science* **5**(1), 16–37.

Roll, E.: 1961, *A History of Economic Thought*, Prentice-Hall, Englewood Cliffs, NJ.

Roscher, W.: 1922, *Grundlagen der Nationalökonomie*, 26th edn, Cotta, Stuttgart.

Rosen, R.: 1987, On complex systems, *European Journal of Operational Research* (30), 129–134.

Rosenberg, N.: 1982, *Inside the black box: Technology and economics*, Cambridge University Press, Cambridge.

Ruvolo, A. and Markus, H.: 1992, Possible selves and performance: The power of self-relevant imagery, *Social Cognition* (9), 95–124.

Sahimi, M.: 1994, *Applications of Percolation Theory*, Taylor & Francis, London.

Saviotti, P. P.: 1996, *Technological Evolution and the Economy*, Edward Elgar, Cheltenham.

Say, J. B.: 1845, *A Treatise on Political Economy*, 4th edn, Grigg & Elliot, Philadelphia.

Schlutz, T. W.: 1971, *Investment in Human Capital*, Free Press, New York.

Schumpeter, J. A.: 1934, *The Theory of Economic Development: An Inquiry into Profits, Capital, Credit, Interest and the Business Cycle, trans. R. Opie in 1934*, Harvard University Press, Cambridge, MA.

Schumpeter, J. A.: 1939a, *Business Cycles*, McGraw-Hill, New York.

Schumpeter, J. A.: 1939b, *Business Cycles I*, Vol. I, McGraw-Hill, New York.

Selgin, G. A.: 2001, Praxeology and understanding: An analysis of the controversy in Austrian ecnomics, *The Review of Austrian Economic* **2**(1), 19–58.

Shackle, G.: 1972, *Epistemics and Economics: A Critique of Economic Doctrines*, Cambridge University Press, Cambridge.

Shionoya, Y.: 1998, Schumpeterian Evolutionism, *in* J. B. Davis, D. W. Hands and U. Mäki (eds), *Handbook of Economic Methodology*, Edward Elgar, Cheltenham, pp. 436–439.

Shrauger, J. S.: 1983, The accuracy of self-predicion: How good are we and why? Paper presented at the Mid-Western Psychological Association.

Simon, H. A.: 1959, Theories of decision-making in economics and behavioral science, *American Economic Review* **49**, 253–283.

Simon, H. A. and Egidi, M.: 1992, *Economics, Bounded Rationality and the Cognitive Revolution*, Elgar, Aldershot.

Smith, P. H.: 1968, *Wheels Within Wheels: A Short History of American Motor Car Manufacturing*, Funk and Wagnalls, New York.

SOC: 1944-1992, *Synthetic Organic Chemicals*, U.S. Government Printing Office, Washington, DC.

Stauffer, D. and Aharony, A.: 1992, *Introduction to Percolation Theory*, 2nd edn, Taylor & Francis, London, Washington.

Stinchcombe, A. L.: 1965, Social structures and organizations, *in* J. G. March (ed.), *Handbook of Organizations*, Rand McNally, Chicago.

Szyperski, N. and Nathusius, K.: 1977, Gründungsmotive und Gründungsvorbehalte – Ergebnisse einer empirischen Studie über potentielle und tatsächliche Unternehmensgründer, *Die Betriebswirtschaft*, Vol. 37, Jena, pp. 299–309.

Thomas': 1905–1993, *Thomas' Register of American Manufacturers*, Thomas Publishing Co., New York.

Thünen, J., H.: 1921, Der isolierte Staat in Beziehung auf Landwirtschaft und Nationalökonomie, Vol. 13, Sammlung sozialwissenschaftlicher Meister, Jena.

Travers, J. and Milgram, S.: 1969, An experimental study of the small world problem, *Sociometry* (32), 425–443.

Turgot, A. R. J.: 1977, *The Economics of A. R. J. Turgot*, Martinus Nihjoff, The Hague.

Urban, G. L. et al.: 1986, Market share rewards to pioneering brands: An empirical analysis and strategic implications, *Management Science* **32**(6), 645–659.

Veblen, T.: 1898, Why is economics not an evolutionary science, *The Quarterly Journal of Economics* **12**.

Viner, J.: 1931, *The Long View and the Short*, The Free Press, Glencoe III.

von Hippel, E.: 1994, Sticky information and the locus of problem solving: Implications for innovation, *Management Science* (40(4)), 420–439.

von Mises, L.: 1959, *Human Action*, William Hodge, London.

von Mises, L.: 1962, *The Ultimate Foundation of Economic Science: An Essay on Method*, Princeton University Press, Princeton, NJ.

Walras, L.: 1954, Elements of pure economics, or the theory of social wealth, *in* G. M. Hodgson (ed.), *Economics and Biology*, Augustus Kelley, New York.

Wasserman, S. and Faust, K.: 1994, *Social Network Analysis: Methods and Applications*, Cambridge University Press, New York.

Wasserman, S. and Galaskiewicz, J.: 1994, *Advances in Social Network Analysis*, Sage Publications, Thousand Oaks, CA.

Weber, M.: 1965, *The Protestant Ethic and the Spirit of Capitalism*, Unwin University Books.

Weinstein, N. D.: 1980, Unrealistic optimism about future life events, *Journal of Personality and Social Psychology* (39), 806–820.

Wernerfelt, B.: 1984, A resource-based view of the firm, *Journal of Strategic Management* (5), 171–180.

Wicksell, K.: 1934, *Lectures on Political Economy*, Vol. 1, trans. E Classen, Macmillan, New York.

Wicksteed, P. H.: 1992, *The Co-ordination of the Laws of Distribution*, Elgar, Aldershot.

Wieser, F. v.: 1927, *Social Economics*, trans. A. F. Hindrichs, Adelphi, New York.

Williamson, O. E.: 1975, *Markets and Hierarchies: Analysis and Antitrust Implications*, Free Press, New York.

Wilson, E. O.: 1998, *Consilience – The Unity of Knowledge*, Knopf, New York.

Witt, U.: 1987, *Individualistische Grundlagen der evolutorischen Ökonomik*, Mohr-Siebeck, Tübingen.

Wolfram, S.: 1996, *The Mathematica Book*, 3rd edn, Wolfram Media/Cambridge Univesity Press, Cambridge.

Zohar, D.: 1990, *The Quantum Self*, Bloomsbury, London.

Index